Riverman

Riverman

the story of

Bus Hatch

Roy Webb

---

foreword by Brad Dimock

FRETWATER ·PRESS·
FLAGSTAFF
ARIZONA
· 2008 ·

Third Edition, revised
©2008 Roy Webb

Fretwater Press
1000 Grand Canyon Avenue
Flagstaff, Arizona 86001
www.fretwater.com

08   09   10   11   12   •   5   4   3   2   1

Library of Congress Control Number: 2008921422
ISBN (cloth) 928-1-892327-03-1
(limited edition of 250)
ISBN (paper) 928-1-892327-02-4

This book was set in Adobe MINION,
P22 Stanyon, and Helvetica Neue 27ULC
designed and typeset in Adobe InDesign
on a Macintosh G4 by Fretwater Press
Printed on permanent acid-free paper

PRIOR PRINTING HISTORY
First Edition: November 1989
(500 softbound)
Second Edition: May 1990
(50 hardbound, 1000 softbound)
ISBN 0-962109-0-4
Labyrinth Publishing
Rock Springs, Wyoming
© 1989 Roy Webb

for Rachel and Sarah

Also by ROY WEBB

IF WE HAD A BOAT: Green River Explorers, Adventurers, and Runners
University of Utah Press • 1986, 1996

CALL OF THE COLORADO
University of Idaho Press • 1994

HIGH, WIDE, AND HANDSOME: The River Journals of Norman D. Nevills
Utah State University Press • 2005

Other river titles from FRETWATER PRESS

THE VERY HARD WAY: Bert Loper and the Colorado River
BRAD DIMOCK • 2007

GLEN CANYON BETRAYED: A Sensous Elegy
KATIE LEE • 2006

THE BRAVE ONES: The 1911–12 River Journals of Emery and Ellsworth Kolb
WILLIAM C. SURAN, editor • 2003

EVERY RAPID SPEAKS PLAINLY: The River Journals of Buzz Holmstrom
BRAD DIMOCK, editor • 2003

SUNK WITHOUT A SOUND: The Tragic Colorado Honeymoon of Glen and Bessie Hyde
BRAD DIMOCK • 2001

THE DOING OF THE THING: The Brief, Brilliant Whitewater Career of Buzz Holmstrom
VINCE WELCH, CORT CONLEY, and BRAD DIMOCK • 1998

Contents

Acknowledgments

I N MANY WAYS, this was a difficult book to write, not because of a dearth of information about Bus, but because of a surfeit. Bus touched so many lives that there are quite literally hundreds of people who still remember him fondly. So the problem for me, as a biographer, was to decide when to draw the line, when I felt I knew enough to stop researching and start writing. I know there are many more people that I could have, and indeed should have, talked to about Bus. Like a boatman at the oars, if there are mistakes made or things left out, those errors are strictly my own.

The first person who deserves thanks is Don Hatch, whose love of his father and sense of his place in the history of river running got this project started in the first place. On a visit to Vernal, while I was working on my first book, I stopped to talk to Don at the Hatch boatyard. We were standing out in the parking lot, literally surrounded by Hatch history, and talking, as we always did, about his father and river history, when Don casually said "I'd sure like to see something written down about my dad." That clicked with me, and all the way home I thought about it; by the time I pulled into my driveway in Salt Lake City, I had resolved to write a biography of Bus Hatch. I learned more about Bus during my conversations with Don than from any other source. And it was not just his reminiscences and memories, nor the many letters, clippings, and photographs that Don dug out of his files that helped so much. Many times, talking to him, I felt like I was talking to Bus. There are differences, of course, in personality, but the real values, the love of the land and of the river, as well as the strong sense of family, came through in every meeting. I was saddened by his passing in 1994, but honored to be asked by the family to speak at his funeral in a standing-room-only church in Vernal.

The same can be said of Ted Hatch, whom I've gotten to know well during the years since this book first came out, and with whom I've had the distinct privilege of sharing the "tea room" on the back of a Hatch rig through the Grand Canyon on a couple of occasions. His stories, his laugh, and the glint in his eye as he spins yet another yarn of the old days also make you think you are sharing a moment with Bus, and can make you forget that you are at the top of Lava Falls. Frank Hatch also allowed me to record his memories of growing up, and provided copies of early family films. Meg Hatch, Don's widow, helped a great deal with photographs and with many other details, and later was the driving force behind collecting and donating the Hatch photographs to the University of Utah, many of which will appear in print for the first time in this edition of *Riverman*. Meg, and her daughter Wendy, as well as many others in the extended Hatch family, have become good friends.

Among the people I interviewed for this book who remembered Bus from Vernal, the best stories came from Duff Swain and Chuck Henderson. Duff's hilarious stories of working on Bus's construction crew really made that aspect of Bus's world come to life, while Chuck Henderson was there at the very beginning of Bus's river career. George Wilkins, Mark Garff, Glade Ross, and Tom Hatch (Bus's grandson) gave me a vivid and fascinating portrait not only of what it was like to work for Bus, but what it was like to be a boatman in those early days of commercial river running. Mark and his wife, Judy, also dug out a number of last-minute photographs. Dave Yeamans, Al Holland, Earl Perry, Jerry "Snake" Hughes, and Cort and Pat Conley all contributed to and reviewed to the chapter on the company's history after Bus's death. Even if they only knew Bus briefly, their comments and memories were invaluable in helping to capture the esprit that came with being a Hatch guide in the 1960s. George T. Henry, who was a Hatch boatman longer than just about anyone, from 1956 until the 1990s, shared some of his memories of the early days and graciously allowed me to use several of his photographs. Warren Herlong answered some questions about the 1967 Grand Canyon trip with the Kennedy family, the answers to which had eluded me elsewhere. Steve Bradley answered many questions, both in person during an interview, and by phone later on, about Bus's early involvement with the Sierra Club during the Echo Park Dam controversy, and how Bus and Lowell Thomas got together for *Search for Paradise*. A real thanks must be said to Fred Washburn and Royce Hatch, whose early interviews with Bus and Cap Mowrey gave me a chance to hear the stories in their own words. As always, Rhoda DeVed of the Thorne Photo Studio was an invaluable source of photos. The staff of the Regional History Room, Uintah County Library, were, as always, helpful and very pleasant to work with. Herm Hoopes, at the time a member of the staff of Dinosaur National Monument, helped by allowing me access to his historical files.

My good friend Mike Brown was with the project from the start, editing each chapter of the 1st edition as it was written, and offering invaluable advice about printing and publishing. He also graciously gave permission for me to work with another publisher for the 3rd edition. The work of Brad Dimock, a "recovering boatman," talented publisher and designer, and noted, award-winning historian of the Colorado River in his own right, has been invaluable in the revision and publication of the 3rd edition and in many other ways as well. I don't think the present volume would have been completed without him.

Finally, I want to thank my wife, Becci. Becci has heard all of my stories about Bus more than once, read the text of the first edition, and provided valuable suggestions. She also let me turn our family vacations into research trips, and in the early days of this project took care of our daughters Rachel and Sarah—both of whom have become avid river runners—while I was off interviewing some old-timer or poking into dusty files. Throughout the year or more that the project initially took, and in the many years since, Becci has provided the love and support that any author needs to complete any book.

ROY WEBB
Salt Lake City, Utah
November 2007

Foreword

HE HISTORY OF RIVER RUNNING on the Green and Colorado is largely homegrown. Although many pioneer boaters came from elsewhere, exotic boats and techniques were largely left behind in favor of those that grew organically along the river itself. Men like Nathaniel Galloway, Bert Loper, Emery and Ellsworth Kolb, Norman Nevills and others built boats and refined techniques based on what worked for them or those that had preceded them. As well, they had a large hand in building the river society as it began to evolve from a few, often egocentric, always eccentric boaters, into a community.

Yet there is a far older boating tradition that somehow got lost along the way—that of the jolly flatboatman of the Ohio and Mississippi. The hard drinking, hard cussing, hard fighting, womanizing scourge of every river town from Pittsburgh to New Orleans. Mike Fink, the most infamous of them all, was called half horse, half alligator. As the 1840s minstrel song recalls,

De boatman dance and de boatman sing, de boatman up to ebryting.
And when de boatman come on shore, dey spend dere money and dey works for more.
When de boatman blows his horn, look out ole man, your daughter's gone.
He stole my sheep, he stole my shoat, Chuck 'em in a bag and tote 'em to de boat.
Dance de boatman, dance. Oh dance de boatman dance.
Dance all night 'til de broad daylight, go home wid de gals in de mornin.

Until the Hatch clan tumbled into the Western river scene it was a remarkably sober, almost humorless crowd. Major Powell tried to look the other way when his cheering men rescued a cask of whiskey from a wrecked boat. Julius Stone on his 1909 expedition finished the trip with the same bottle of whiskey he began it with—still unopened. Norman Nevills was a famous tetotaller and often groused in his diary about any unbecoming behavior amongst the crew. Clyde Eddy blew his tin whistle each morning to roust his men—and when he felt morale slipping, the best booster he could come up with was to shave. For most early boaters, river running was serious business and nothing to be toyed with, laughed at, or celebrated.

Look out, boys, here come the Hatches. Bus Hatch, his cousin Frank Swain, and their many brothers, inlaws, and outlaws, all loved to scrap, to drink, to have a good time, often at the expense of meticulous boating or fine cuisine. In fact, their very inspiration to begin boating came from jailed Parley Galloway, the errant ne'er-do-well son of the more straight-laced pioneer boatman Nathaniel Galloway. Even though Parley shirked his promise to teach Hatch and Swain the finer arts of whitewater, the Hatch clan figured it out themselves, hammering together a few boats and careening down the rapids of Dinosaur. One wonders, in fact, how much Galloway could have taught the impatient, irreverant cousins had he not skipped town. The tale of Bus Hatch walking into Green River from a boat trip to resupply food and returning to the boats with a bag of bullets and beer, typifies how serious the men were about precision endeavors. As do the flippant names they painted on their boats in 1934: *What Next?*, *Don't Know*, *Who Cares*. One can picture the rest of the boating world bristling.

When Bus passed his company on to sons Don and Ted, that wild ethic— that errant spore of the feisty flatboatman—went with it. If it wasn't a good time, why go? And the men they recruited to run boats for them took that to heart. The tales of Dennis Massey, Brett Reddy, Jimmy Hall, pounding each other to pieces, drinking the well dry, grabbing the gals, forgetting to cook dinner, would scandalize any modern outfitter. But that's how it went for a while. When the National Park Service in the 1980s decided to implement a draconian alcohol policy, Ted Hatch laughed at one boatman's meeting, saying, "I don't think I could *run* Lava Falls if I wasn't three sheets to the wind!" Don Hatch joked about the Hatch legacy once saying, "Those boys probably set back boating twenty years!"

The heyday soon passed, of course, as it had to. The Hatch River Expeditions of today is as safe, professional, and ethical as any you'll find.

But the innoculum of chaos they brought to the river cannot be undone. And thank heaven for that. Throughout the 1960s, '70s, and '80s the celebratory ethic spread throughout the river community—never again achieving the high (low) points of Mike Fink or Dennis Massey—but instead instilling a sense of joy and freedom on the river that is a key element of the river experience. Bus Hatch taught us not to take ourselves so damned seriously.

River running today is a multi-million dollar industry, and the days of grabbing someone from the drunk tank to run a boat are fortunately resigned to folklore. Even so, it is good to look back now and then and see where we came from. In this Roy Webb has done us a great service. His tale of how a fun-loving carpenter from Vernal, Utah, grew to become a seminal figure in the world of river running is a critical piece of the larger picture. And a damned fun piece too.

Dance, boatmen, dance.

BRAD DIMOCK
2008

Introduction

I T'S NOT HOW LONG YOU LIVE, it's what you accomplish while you're here. This was part of Bus Hatch's philosophy, and these were some of his parting words when he died. He was sharply critical, quick to protest and condemn, yet fast to forgive and forget. He loved and hated all within the same minute. His pace was fast and furious. "Do something, even if it's wrong!" he often said. "Don't just stand there like you're getting milked," he'd shout. Since he was a perfectionist he should have died much younger, but he didn't die until he accomplished all the goals he set in life.

A prominent goal was to navigate by boat the whitewater rivers of the West, and even of the world. His boating skill matched and beat the best of his time. His first time accomplishments place him as a captain among his peers: first to navigate the Indus River in Pakistan, among the first fifty through the Grand Canyon, among the first to run the Middle Fork of the Salmon, first to take a woman—his wife, Eva—down the Yampa River, among the first hundred to successfully navigate Cataract Canyon. He was also a pioneer of mass transport with rubber boats in the late 1940s, and certainly the first to introduce the members of the Sierra Club to the beauties to be found in his own back yard, the canyons of the Green and Yampa Rivers. Without Bus Hatch, Echo Park Dam would certainly have been built, Dinosaur National Monument would have been flooded, and the control of the National Park Service lands taken over by the Bureau of Reclamation.

All who knew Bus Hatch admired him. His many friends love him; his few enemies feared him. A man among men? Yes. The late Clyde Eddy, pioneer river runner of the 1920s, said of Bus that he was "without equal in the tough places." Bus was without equal because his perfectionist style seemed to place him above mortal being. His sharp mind and leadership will never be forgotten.

DON HATCH
1989

CONFLICT MAKES NEWS, and news makes history; yet men live rich and quiet lives outside the boiling currents of their times, and who shall say whether the thousand existences in quiet do not more clearly express the shape of human experience than the fiercely spotlighted existence that survives as history.

— DALE MORGAN

Early Days

VERNAL, UTAH, in 1902 was a sleepy little farm town. The dusty streets were lined with cottonwood trees, watered by the irrigation ditches that were common to all Mormon towns. Vernal had been settled by the Church of Jesus Christ of Latter-day Saints—(LDS, or Mormons)—scarcely twenty years before, and in that short time the town had already been through one Indian scare, shortly after settlement, and periodic bouts of boosterism, with local promoters trying to promote a railroad to connect the town with Salt Lake City, almost 200 miles to the west, or with other lines in western Colorado. But nothing much had come of either the scare or the dreams, and the routines of small town life went on unchanged by the world outside the Ashley Valley.

The valley was a favorite place for settlement long before the Mormons came in 1878. The ancient, enigmatic Fremont people had lived there a thousand years before, and vanished, leaving only arrowheads and flint chips, eagerly sought by local collectors, and many beautiful and mysterious rock carvings and drawings on the walls of nearby canyons. Later, the Uintah Utes, one of several bands of the tribe that occupied western Colorado and eastern Utah, called the valley home during the long, sometimes harsh winters. There was plenty of game, wood, and feed for their horses, and the valley was sheltered from all but the worst of winter storms. During the hot summers, the Utes roamed the mountains that bounded the valley north and south. The Utes were hunters and gatherers, and were known as fierce warriors, excellent horsemen, and good shots with bow or rifle. They were a handsome people, and delighted in dressing in fine buckskins and beadwork.

Later came the fur trappers, who spilled over the Uinta Mountains into the Ashley Valley. They only passed though the area, or wintered there occasionally, but the valley was named for one of the first trappers, William Ashley, who passed through the valley via the Green River in 1825, and gave his name to one of the most-feared rapids on the upper river, Ashley Falls. The valley was a beautiful place; lush—especially compared to the surrounding desert, which, in the words of a scout sent by Brigham Young in the 1850s, was good only "to hold the world together"—well-watered, full of tall grass and trees, with rich soil, it was the oasis of the Uinta Basin. The basin itself was a broad, mostly arid valley drained by the Green River and its tributaries, surrounded on all sides by high mountains. On the south was the Tavaputs Plateau, locally known as the Book Cliffs. A remote and uninhabited area even today, the Tavaputs Plateau was a favorite hunting ground for the Utes from earliest times. To the north were the Uinta Mountains, tall, forested, a land of glacial lakes and sweeping meadows. From them came Ashley Creek, the stream that gave Ashley Valley its water, its trees, its life.

Although it didn't flow directly through Vernal, the nearby Green River was a dominant fact of life in the Uinta Basin. From its start in the distant Wind River Mountains of Wyoming to the north, the Green ran through wild canyons and unpopulated valleys before dramatically entering the basin at the mouth of Split Mountain Canyon. Once out into the basin, the river rested from its hurried course above, looping a hundred miles through the valley in sinuous, cottonwood-lined curves. The thrifty Mormons depended on farming, but the bottoms along the river were also an important source of food for the people of Vernal. The marshes swarmed with thousands of geese, ducks, and other waterfowl during their annual migrations, and herds of deer, antelope, and occasionally elk came to drink from the muddy waters.

While it was important as a source of game, the river could also turn deadly. Ice jams clogged it in the winter, causing severe flooding. In the spring, the annual rise could overtop the banks, washing away irrigation ditches, fields, and even houses that were too near the river. Even worse, more than one family lost a brother, a father, or a friend in the swirling brown waters. Children were forbidden to play near the river, making it an irresistible magnet, indeed a paradise, for all the boys of the area. They hunted and fished the tree-lined banks, and swam in the calm stretches. As much fun as the river bottoms were, though, it was the canyons above—mysterious, moody, dark, unpenetrated—that stirred their imaginations. Even the names of the canyons had a mysterious, enticing ring to them: Flaming Gorge, the Canyon of Lodore, Whirlpool Canyon. But few people in Vernal ever ventured out onto the river itself, save to cross it on the Maube or Alhandra ferries.

After a couple of false starts, the first Mormon settlers entered Ashley Valley in November 1878, led by Jeremiah Hatch. Jeremiah, or "Uncle Jerry" as he came to be known, was a native of Vermont who joined the Mormon church in 1839[1]. He endured all the trials of the unsettled period of the 1840s, and moved to the Salt Lake Valley in September 1850. There his skills as a blacksmith were badly needed, but Brigham Young and the other church leaders soon found another use for Jeremiah. It turned out that he got along very well with the Indians of the area, who were in a constant state of unease over the increasing encroachment of their lands by Mormon settlers. As a consequence, Jeremiah was shuttled all over Utah, putting out first this fire and then that, calming settlers and Indians alike. In the years before he settled in the Ashley Valley, he lived in Lehi, Manti, Smithfield, and Heber City.

The winter of 1878-79 was known among early settlers of Vernal as the "hard winter." Snow came early and stayed late, and many of that first band of settlers died during a diphtheria epidemic brought on by cold and hunger. Jeremiah and his sons made several arduous trips over the Uintas to bring back supplies from Wyoming. Nor were their troubles solely caused by the elements. That same year, after the Meeker Massacre in Colorado, there was a brief Indian scare that caused the settlers to "fort up" for protection, building walls between cabins to create a stockade. The fort on the east end of town was centered around Jeremiah Hatch's cabin, and came to be known as Hatchtown, but it was never really needed; after a conference among Ute leaders held in front of Jeremiah's cabin, the scare died down. His fellow settlers wanted to call the new settlement Hatch, in his honor, but Jeremiah settled the matter, declaring that the town would henceforth be known as Vernal[2].

Jeremiah Hatch

After the death of his first wife in 1869, Jeremiah somehow found time to marry young Aurilla Hadlock, whom he had met (and converted) while on a mission to the eastern U.S. in 1870. Also a native of Vermont, Aurilla was born in 1852. She accompanied Jeremiah to the Ashley Valley in 1878. In 1887, Aurilla went to Salt Lake City for training at the LDS hospital as a midwife. Thereafter, she was a common sight in the valley as she galloped off on her big black horse Nig to assist at the birth of another baby. When the LDS Church asked Jeremiah to move to Moab, Utah, in 1892, she followed him. [3]

Jeremiah and Aurilla had nine children. Their fourth child, and the second son, was Solon Franklin, named for an uncle who had died in the Civil War. Solon quickly shed his first name and was always known as Frank. Frank Hatch was born in Heber City on October 22, 1877, and so was still a baby when the family moved to Vernal. He grew up to be a handsome man, tall and dark, with jet-black hair and chiseled features. In fact, it was said that when he dressed in his purple satin shirt, he could be mistaken for an Indian, and one characteristic Frank shared with his father was his ease in dealing with Indians. The Utes were always welcome at the Hatch homestead on the eastern end of Vernal, and Frank often visited on the Ute Reservation near Fort Duchesne.

Unlike his father, however, Frank was not one to spend much time in town attending to civic, religious, or family responsibilities. He preferred to roam the mountains surrounding Vernal, prospecting for minerals. Frank always had another claim, another big strike, over the next hill. He would come into town with his pockets loaded with ore samples, or when he was forced by his duties as watermaster to remain in Vernal, he would have sheepherders bring him in samples. None of them ever panned out, but that didn't stop him. It was the looking more than anything else that attracted him.

Frank had his own sense of responsibility, though. While prospecting around the Green River north of Vernal, Frank met Albert Williams, a black man who had been the camp keeper for the notorious Wild Bunch outlaw gang of Browns Park, and later lived as a hermit in Little Hole. The two men became friends. When "Speck," as he was known because of a skin condition that left him with a mottled, or speckled appearance, came down with his last illness in 1934, Frank took him in and cared for him in the Hatch home until he died. Some of the citizens of Vernal grumbled about Frank having a black man in his house, but Frank ignored them, and saw to it that his friend had a proper burial in the Rock Point cemetery.

Another time, two prisoners escaped from sheriff Lafe Richardson while they were being transferred from the Uintah County jail. They headed for

the east end of town, in the direction of Frank's house. When he found out what the commotion was about, he grabbed his old double-barrel shotgun, despite his sixty years, and rounded up the first two men he saw and held them at gunpoint. Unfortunately, they turned out to be not the escaped prisoners, but two neighbors who had showed up to see what was going on. The two prisoners were later found to be hiding in the basement of a house being built by Cap Mowrey.

Frank became the city watermaster in 1910, and was put in charge of inspecting the all-important irrigation ditches and canals. The authority granted him as watermaster, however, belied the job's actual responsibilities. Unless there was a major break in a canal, or a dispute over water between two farmers, all he had to do was walk or ride along the ditch banks, looking for problems. Frank always carried a telescoping steel fishing pole, and seldom came home without his pockets full of fish, even the little ones that most fishermen would throw back. When he wasn't inspecting canals or prospecting, Frank spent most of his time socializing. He would put on his suit and stroll downtown, to visit with his cronies at the Commercial Hotel on Main Street. If anything bad could be said of Frank Hatch, one of Vernal's best-liked and most-respected citizens, it was that he didn't like to work very hard.

Frank preferred to leave that to his long-suffering wife, Julianna Swain Hatch, known simply as Annie. Annie was born in Salt Lake City, and married Frank in Vernal in 1899. In many ways, Annie was Frank's opposite. Of Swedish ancestry, she was blonde and fair-skinned, with blue eyes. She was musical, as

Frank
Hatch
with
Ted
Hatch
circa
1935

Julianna
Swain
Hatch

were all the Swains, with a beautiful voice. Where Frank was usually gruff and aloof with his children, Annie was devoted to her family, loving and even indulgent. She never complained when Frank would bring home three, five, or a dozen guests, nor when the Utes would set up their teepees and camp out in her front yard during the annual rodeo in the summer. As the *Vernal Express* wrote in her eulogy when she died in 1937, "The home over which she presided as hostess, was often noted for its hospitality, a place where often the entire neighborhood gathered." [4]

Frank and Annie had four boys, Robert Rafael, Alton, Justus Valoy, Corwin Lamont, and a single girl, Thelma. In the style of the times, they all were soon known not by their given names but by nicknames. Justus Valoy, for instance, was known variously as Bay, Fat, or Tiny; Alton was Alt, Buck, or Bishop, and Corwin, the youngest child, became Tom. Thelma, the one girl, was inevitably known as "Sis." All of them had distinct personalities, different from the others. Bay was like his father, easy-going and friendly. "He never had an enemy in the world," Duff Swain remembers. "He liked everybody and everything tickled him and he woke up happy and he went to bed happy." Alton was the businessman of the family, always more ambitious and hard-working. When the others found time to hunt and fish, Alt was usually working, first

for a local butcher and later for the J.C. Penney store on Main Street. Tom, the youngest, was articulate and literate, and later went to college at Brigham Young University, as did Alt. Thelma, as the only girl in the family, had the rest of them wrapped around her finger[5]. She was the only one of them who could boss her eldest brother around and get away with it. What they all shared was a very real sense of family. What affected one affected all, good or bad. This applied equally to their double cousins, the Swains, of whom more later.

The one who grew up the least like his easy-going father was the oldest, born on April 20, 1902. He was christened Robert Rafael, but he soon became known simply as Bus.[6] Bus shared his father's black hair, but there the resemblance ended. Bus had a ruddy complexion, and was prone to sunburn. He was of medium height and weight. Bus also had his father's high cheekbones, a feature which gave him some trouble later in life, when he had to sand down his shotgun stocks in order to shoot. The most striking difference, however, was not physical. Unlike Frank, Bus was impatient, quick-tempered, a perfectionist. Bus had lightning-quick reflexes, and often became frustrated when his actions couldn't keep up with his thoughts. Bus never walked when he could run, never hesitated when he could act. Bus would "bounce out of bed on the dead run in the morning and never shut it off until he went to sleep at night."[7] He had little time for those less adept than he was at anything, and yet Bus could command fierce loyalty from his family and friends, and those who knew him. Later his employees would strive to their utmost to please him. He was generous with time, money, or the shirt off his back. He was always ready with a laugh or a joke, and was quick to make friends. He loved to play practical jokes, although he didn't like them played on him. As quickly as he blew up at someone, he was over it. He mixed well in any crowd, and many people that he considered acquaintances thought of him as their best friend. Above all, Bus was a man with no pretenses, and he refused to tolerate pretense in others.

Bus's early education was at the Wilcox Academy, a local school run by the Vernal Congregational church. His mother washed clothes to pay her children's tuition, which with fees and other expenses could add up to almost $100 a year for all the boys, a princely sum in those days. Bus was a good, quick student, and his grades were always straight A's. He had a natural talent for both math and languages, and learned to speak French and Latin at the school. Later, when he was a teenager, he taught at the school for a short time. In 1920, Bus enrolled at the University of Utah, but stayed only one quarter before he quit school and returned to Vernal. Not that he wasn't a good student, but his interests lay elsewhere, and he still had younger brothers and a sister at home to help support.

Like most children in turn-of-the-century Utah, Bus was at least nominally a member of the Mormon church. However, none of the family ever took religion very seriously. Duff Swain described one early attempt to baptize some of the boys:

> When they got to baptizing somebody, they'd usually take you out to the creek or the canal or somewhere. [The Bishop] decided that this bunch of hellions should be baptized. He got out there in the water, about up to his waist, and my mother and aunt [Annie Hatch] started to run these kids down and dragging them out there and he was baptizing them, see. He baptized my brother Frank [Swain], and when they took after Garn [Swain] and Bay [Hatch], they headed off bare-footed down through an alfalfa patch and they outran my mother and my aunt and they got away, and they never did get baptized. I believe my mother and Aunt Annie just give up on 'em at that point.

Annie's attempts to instill religious training in Bus met with no better success. One time she did get him to sacrament meeting at the local ward. When the

Bus Hatch circa 1920

Vernal baseball team circa 1925. Bus standing far left; Alt next uniformed player; Tom third from right; Bay kneeling second from left

tray was passed to him, Bus gobbled all the bread in the tray, drank all the water from the sacrament cup at a gulp, and said "Jesus Christ, Ma, is that all they're gonna give us to eat around here?" Bus never went to church after that, but he never discouraged his own children from attending. Later in life, when he was a successful contractor, Bus would take on remodeling jobs for any of the local churches, Mormon or not, often for free or for a nominal fee.

Bus and his brothers grew up with their double cousins, the Swains.[8] Bus's father, Frank Hatch married Annie Swain; her brother, Enoch, or Nick, as he was known, married Frank's sister Florence. The two families might as well have been one big bunch of brothers, for the Swains had five boys: Frank, Gilbert, Garn, Shelby, and Karl. Like their Hatch cousins, the Swain boys went not by their real names but by nicknames. Frank, the eldest, was Hush; next was Gilbert, known as Gib and later Pete; then Garn Advance, who was known as Magpie, shortened to Maggie, and Karl, who was always known as Duff. When Thelma Hatch married Royce Mowrey, a local man (soon known as Cap or Monk), the number of men in the extended family was an even ten.

The "outlaws," as they liked to call themselves, did everything together. Bus, Bay, Alt, and Frank Swain were all on the Vernal baseball team in the 1920s. Bus, with his quick reflexes and speed, was a good infielder, while Bay was known as a home run hitter. The cousins roamed the mountains and river bottoms around Vernal as a group, hunting and fishing. Bus and the boys always had some new project, some new thing to try out. It might have

been hunting in a new area, or playing a joke on Uncle Abner Swain or Hen Lee, a retired outlaw who lived in LaPoint, west of Vernal. Or it might have been making a new batch of the moonshine they called "sideswipe," because it would make you "see double and feel single." And they defended each other against any and all comers. They might fight among themselves, but if an outsider picked a fight with one of them, he picked it with the entire family.[9]

From an early age, Bus took on more and more of the responsibility of providing for the family. As the eldest, he was expected to help support not only his own growing family but his younger brothers and his sister. Given his father's inclination to roam the hills or socialize with his friends instead of supporting his wife and children, Bus had little choice. When he was fifteen, Bus, following in his grandfather's footsteps, began a career as a builder. He started out working for a local contractor, Lije Campbell, for three dollars a day. Lije had no training in building, but he had been to "guessing school" and could estimate by looking at a job about how much it would cost. Bus, who was very good in math, soon took over the bidding process, figuring how much materials were needed, how much labor would cost, how to build in profits, and so on. Soon Bus could look at a job and tell within three two-by-fours how much it would cost to build, and give Lije a comprehensive bid. After two or three years working for Lije Campbell, Bus started his own contracting business. When he was just sixteen, Bus built his first house, on the corner of 4th North and 2nd East in Vernal, for his parents.

Like everything else the Hatches and Swains did, building soon became a family affair. Bus would figure the jobs and the bid, lay out the foundation, and do the framing—he was too impatient for finish carpentry—and then be the boss for the rest of the job. Garn and Shelby Swain and Bay Hatch were plasterers and stonemasons, and Cap Mowrey did wiring and plumbing. Duff Swain and Tom Hatch, being the youngest members of their respective families, did odd jobs such as lathe and shingle work, digging basements, and pouring cement. Once a building was finished, they would all pitch in together and paint it. The Swains ran a brickyard outside of town, where Steinaker Reservoir is now, and made their own bricks. On the Hatch homestead, they had their own gypsum vats, where they boiled gypsum to make their own plaster. From start to finish, they were a self-contained family construction business.

Bus was soon in great demand as a builder, for he could be relied onto build a house quickly and do a good job. In a letter written to Alt in 1927, Bus noted that they had "about ten times more work than we can handle right now." Bus and various members of his family built many of the buildings in Vernal over the next several decades: the Central School, the Safeway store, the Chevron bulk plant; the bus depot, the *Vernal Express* building, the municipal swimming pool, the old cobblerock gas station that used to stand on the corner of Vernal Avenue and Main Street, and most of the houses in the east end of town.[10] When there wasn't enough work in Vernal, they would build buildings in other towns, such as the Catholic Church in Roosevelt, and the Deep Creek School

Bus Hatch on the transit

Bus Hatch's house, built circa 1929

At other times, Bus built buildings in Salt Lake City, Lark and Bingham, Utah, near the copper mines, and in Colorado. They also found time to build houses for themselves. In 1927, Bus, Cap, Bay and Garn Swain bought a lot south of the old Hatch homestead in the east end of Vernal. In the next few years, they all helped each other build houses on the lot, and built them in such a way that they didn't have to hire any outside contractors. Most of them lived near each other all of their lives. All of the houses are still standing.[11]

All of their early jobs were done with hand tools—there were no power saws or backhoes in those days. Boards were sawed by hand, cement was mixed and poured by hand, basements were dug with shovels. But Bus's contracts were always finished under bid and ahead of schedule. Bus never walked while on the job—if he needed a hammer or other tool, he would trot over to get it, not walk, and he expected those who worked for him to do the same.

But sometimes his impatience could bring unexpected results. In 1930, while building the Shell gas station that stood on the corner of First West and Main Street in Vernal, they had to dig holes to accommodate two 9,000 gallon gas tanks. After digging down about a foot and a half with pick and shovel they struck a layer of hard clay that stopped them cold. Duff Swain recalls what happened next:

> You could dig for an hour and you couldn't get a wheelbarrow full of that out. I called Bus over and I said "Bus, there's just no way we're going to dig the son of a bitch this summer. We're going to grow old digging this. [Bus] got down

in there and hit that a couple of licks with a pick and said "By God, Duff, you're right, there's no way. Let's shoot the son of a bitch."

They drilled a small hole, got some dynamite and blasting caps from Ray Ashton's store, and stuffed the sticks down in the hole. As they got ready to blast, however, Duff began to have second thoughts, as this was right in the middle of town on a summer day:

> "This is gonna blow dirt all over hell, maybe blow rocks and break some windows or something, Bus." And he says, "We'll cover the son of a bitch up," and we had a great iron wheelbarrow, just one of these great big construction wheelbarrows. We lit that fuse and turned that wheelbarrow upside down on top of that hole. That shot went off and that wheelbarrow went way up about three hundred yards and come down just as round as a keg.

A Mrs. Gibson, who owned a hotel across the street, had in the meanwhile been watching these proceedings with a jaundiced eye. Duff remembers her as having "whiskers on her chin, [and she was] just mean as a wolf" When the shot went off,

> A boulder come out of that hole just about the size of a football and went right straight across the street, and this old lady Gibson was standing on her front porch. The goddamn rock sailed over her head, just about a foot above that plate glass window, and tore a hole in there you could run a bull through. It went right through the lobby and wound up in the back of the garage. That old lady jumped in the air about two feet and clicked her heels together; she called us about everything that you could call a white man.

A few feet lower and it would have hit Mrs. Gibson "right in the breadbasket," which "probably would have been a good thing for the community," they concluded. Needless to say, work on the service station was delayed while they fixed up her hotel.[12]

But for all his impatience, Bus knew when to take time off. While building the Safeway store on Main street, for instance, under a hot summer sky, a friend stopped by to show off the trout he had caught in the Uintas. "Jesus Christ," Bus said, throwing down his tools, "enough's enough. Boys, we're going fishing." After several days in the mountains, they came back to work and finished the job, still on time and under bid.[13]

Bus's true love was always the outdoors. He and his brothers and cousins spent all their spare time hunting deer in the mountains above town, geese and ducks in the marshes by Stewart Lake, or fishing in Brush Creek or Ashley Creek. Nor was this just a pastime. Times were hard in the late 1920s and early '30s, in Vernal as everywhere else. The game and fish they brought home was a very real part of the family's diet. If the hunting wasn't good in Utah, they would drift over into nearby Colorado and poach a deer or two. Poaching didn't carry the stigma that it does today, and Bus and his family, like many others, poached for food, not for trophies. Everything they shot or caught was used; it was unthinkable to waste game or fish.

That didn't mean they didn't have occasional run-ins with the local game wardens, but they were usually able to keep any encounter with the law from becoming a problem, as Duff Swain remembered:

> [W]e didn't let the game wardens bother us too much. You know, the game warden would come around, we'd have a leg of meat hanging up, we'd tell him we cut it off a buck we shot a few days before, invite him in and feed him a bunch of that doe meat, and some potatoes and gravy, give him a drink of whiskey and send [him] on his way.[14]

More than just a source of food, however, hunting and fishing was a great joy

Riverma

and inspiration for Bus. When Bus was up in the Uintas, he would often stop just to admire a beautiful sunset or a particularly striking scene. In the woods or the canyons, there was no pretense, no deception. Bus was never more at home than with his shotgun down by Stewart Lake, or fishing on Brush Creek in the Uintas. Nature was his religion, the outdoors his church. He never felt the need for any other. And he was a tireless hunter. In a letter to Alt Hatch, Bus described one hunting trip in October, 1927. In the course of a day, he walked almost twenty miles, over the rugged country south of the Green River near Little Hole. During that day he shot, cleaned, and hauled back to camp three deer of his own; between him and the rest of the party, they brought home nine deer to add to the family larder.

During the winter months, hunting geese and ducks along the Green River was their favorite diversion. Duff Swain recalled one goose-hunting trip that had an unexpected ending:

Cap Mowrey was always getting some kind of gadget. Goose calls come out about this time, and I don't know, he paid four or five dollars for this goose call and he practiced and practiced and practiced and then he'd listen to geese, you know, and he'd practice. He got this down to where he was pretty damned good. So we all got down to Stewart's Lake, down just south of Jensen. We got down there 'fore daylight and set some decoys out and got hunkered down in those wet cattails. Pretty soon here come a herd of geese. Bus says "Monk! Get on that goose call. Get on that goose call!" Old Cap reached in his hunting coat pocket and got that goose call out and put it up and let the by-damnedest squawl out of it you ever heard and them geese just turned around and headed out of the county. Tracy [Bus] jumped up, was gonna shoot him, Bay and Garn got him and took his shotgun away from him. Oh, he was mad enough to kill him. [Bus said] "I'll shoot you, you son of a bitch, you practice six months, let one blat out of that and scared every goose out of Uintah County." Cap says "I can't figure out what went wrong." [Bus] says "If anything could go wrong, you goggle-eyed bastard, it would."

As it turned out, some .22 rifle shells in the pocket of Cap's hunting jacket had gotten into the goose call. Duff concluded that the call "just flat broke up that goose hunt right there."

Bus, Bay, Cap, and other members of the family belonged to the local rod and gun club, and Bus loved to compete in shooting and trapshooting matches. He was a crack shot, and often brought home trophies and prizes. When he was hunting with his sons, though, he would always give them the first shot. Bus used a lever-action .250-3000 Savage rifle. Hunting in the Uintas one time, they flushed a deer, and Bus fired shot after shot as fast as he could work the lever. When asked why he was shooting so fast, he replied, "By God, there's danger where there's lead a-flying. I'll build a lead fence and let the son of a bitch run into it." He was also an excellent shot with a shotgun. Don Hatch recalls the time he shot six ducks on the wing with a pump shotgun. Bus hit the last duck before the first had hit the ground.

When they weren't hunting for geese or deer, Bus and his brothers and cousins were fishing. The streams near Vernal abounded with fish, and it was not uncommon for each of them to bring home their limit of trout. As a member of the rod and gun club, Bus was on the fish committee, and helped pack thousands of fingerlings into the Uintas by truck and horseback to stock the many lakes.

Another source of both food and income, not to mention a good time, was seining.[15] The Green River, about twelve miles east of Vernal, was full of fish. At the urging of a local old-timer, "Uncle" Ike Burton, Bus bought a 150-foot seine, or net. They would take the seine to the mouth of Split Mountain Canyon, anchor one end of the net on shore, and take the other end out into the river in a boat. Then the net was drawn in, bringing in hundreds of fish. They would repeat this process several times a day, even when the river was running cold and full from spring run-off. Often the weight of the fish would tear holes in the cotton fabric of the net, and then they would have to stand around in the cold while they repaired the seine. The best fish they kept for family fish fries; the rest were given to poor families or sold for chicken feed. Uncle Ike would supervise from the bank meanwhile, a jug of moonshine in his hand.

To get out into the river with the seine, they needed a boat. Neither Bus nor any of his family had ever built a boat before, but such things never stopped Bus—he could build anything out of wood. In one of the shops on the Hatch yard, they built a small open skiff, about twelve feet long, and narrow of beam. Their first try didn't work very well, but Bus always learned from his mistakes, and the second attempt was more successful. They used the little boat for years, taking out and hauling in the big cotton net.

For Bus, as he rowed the little boat out with the seine, the looming mouth of Split Mountain Canyon was an irresistible challenge. He had been often been to Echo Park, and hiked down into Jones Hole, in Whirlpool Canyon, to fish for trout. But what was it really like in those gloomy depths? Local legend had it that the canyons were impassable, that there were cataracts and whirlpools, known as "sucks," which would destroy any boat. Everyone in Vernal knew the stories about the Canyon of Lodore: John Wesley Powell had lost a boat there in 1869, and others had reportedly disappeared trying to float the river.[16] The river couldn't be run, the local wise men said, and anyone foolish enough to try would be washed out, a corpse. To someone like Bus, for whom the phrase "it can't be done" was a personal affront, that was enough. He would give it a try.

e n d n o t e s

[1] Another descendant of Jeremiah Hatch is Utah Senator Orrin Hatch, who is a great-grandson. Thus Senator Hatch and Ted Hatch, one of Bus's sons, are second cousins.

[2] The Hatch River Expeditions boat yard still occupies this same land, and one of the original cabins is still in existence.

[3] Like most Mormon patriarchs of the 19th century, Jeremiah was reputed to have had several wives. It is reported that he had over 30 children. One of the wives was a Ute Indian woman from the nearby reservation, but the identities of the others are

not presently known. Jeremiah died in May 1903 in Vernal; Aurilla in January 1926. Information about them comes from their respective obituaries in the *Vernal Express*, and from family histories found in the Ashley Valley D.U.P. papers, University of Utah Libraries Special Collections.

4   "Wife of Water Superintendent Dies at Hospital," *Vernal Express*, 29 July 1937. p. 1

5   Thelma—which was pronounced "The-Elma"—was also the delicate one of the family. She was always ill, always fascinated with death, and for many years claimed to be at death's door. Ironically, she outlived all of her brothers and her husband, and died in 1985

6   The origin of the name "Bus" seems to be lost to history. None of the persons I interviewed could tell me where the name came from. When he got older, Bus had his name legally changed from Robert to Bus. One theory was that since Bus was always in a hurry, he tended to break things, and thus was known as "Buster," shortened to "Bus." Another nickname for Bus among the family was "Tracy," but again, no one seems to know the origin of this name. All of the spellings were the family's own.

7   Karl "Duff" Swain interview, 13 November 1987.

8   IBID.

9   IBID. Nick Swain, Frank's father, was the deputy sheriff, and this was during Prohibition, so the boys were forced to make their own moonshine. Local legend has it that they took over a still hidden in Split Mountain Canyon, after its original operator was arrested by the sheriff. This led to the name Moonshine Draw, and Moonshine Rapid.

10   "Bus Hatch Rites Held Tuesday in Vernal 1st Ward," *Vernal Express*, 22 June 1967. The cobblerock gas station, torn down in the 1970s, was recently rebuilt in the same location and serves as a focus for city events.

11   The house that Cap Mowrey built for Thelma was used by Hatch River Expeditions as an office for many years, and the house that Bus and Eva lived in, across the street, was used by Ted Hatch as the office for his Grand Canyon river expeditions until 2007.

12   Karl "Duff" Swain interview, 13 November 1987

13   Ted Hatch interview, 13 March 1988.

14   Karl "Duff" Swain interview, 13 November 1987.

15   IBID.

16   Frank Goodman and Jack Sumner, both of whom had been with Powell on his 1869 expedition, later settled in Vernal. Goodman died in 1915, and is buried in the Vernal cemetery. "Vernal Memorial Park Rendezvous for Many Great River Runners" The *Vernal Express*, 22 July 1971.

Now We're Safe, Now We're On The River

Bus's COUSIN Frank Swain, like his father Nick Swain, was a deputy sheriff for Uintah County. In September, 1929, a woman named Loretta Luck came to Frank and swore out a warrant for her husband, whom she claimed had abandoned her and her children. When the man was arrested and jailed in LaSal, Utah, a small town near Moab, Frank went down to pick him up.[1] The prisoner turned out to be Parley Galloway, whose father, Nathaniel, was already something of a legend in Vernal. In the late 1880s, Nathaniel, or Than, as his friends called him, began running the canyons of the Green and Colorado Rivers, prospecting and trapping beaver. He used boats of his own design, light, flat-bottomed skiffs that were very maneuverable.

More importantly, though, he used them in a way that had never been tried. Rather than row with his back to the current, the traditional way to handle a boat, Galloway turned his boat around, facing downstream, so he could see where he was going and use his oars to control the boat in the roughest water. Nathaniel used his little craft and his revolutionary technique to run the Green, the Yampa, and even the Colorado in its most difficult stretches, Cataract Canyon and the Grand Canyon. Sometimes with a partner, but most often alone, he traveled regions that just a few scant years earlier were the haunts only of outlaws and hermits. Before his death in 1913, Galloway had spent more time on the Colorado River than any other man, and was known as the premier riverman of his time.

Parley Galloway

Frank Swain

Parley learned how to build and run river boats, literally at his father's knee, taking many trips with Nathaniel down the Green and its turbulent tributaries. When he was just a teenager, he and his father ran the Green from Vernal to the confluence with the Colorado, and back up the latter to Moab. In 1909, they ran the Yampa together on the spring flood. Parley successfully guided the Clyde Eddy party through Cataract Canyon and the Grand Canyon in 1927, even though he had never been down the Grand Canyon. On that trip, with a crew composed of inexperienced, "pink-wristed collegians," and an equally inexperienced leader, Parley was "the glue that held the group together," in one historian's phrase. So his river credentials were without question. His ethics, however, were another matter.

During long conversations with Parley in his cell in the Uintah County jail, Bus and Frank listened eagerly to Parley's tales of the deep canyons of the Green and the Colorado—as Bus later put it, they spent as much time in jail as Parley did. Both Bus and Frank had read John Wesley Powell's account of his pioneering river voyages, and they were fascinated by the idea of navigating the river. Sensing opportunity in Frank and Bus's interest, Parley told the cousins that if they would collect some money Clyde Eddy owed to him, and bail him out, he would help them build a Galloway boat and then guide them down the river. Bus and Frank agreed, and bailed Parley out of jail. He thereupon did "what he should have done, he skipped out," and promptly disappeared from the Uinta Basin, seldom to be seen again in eastern Utah.[2] The two cousins were undeterred, however. They had built a boat once, and could do it again. As for the running the river through the mysterious canyons, by God, they would just do it on their own.

Bus and Frank were not unfamiliar with the Green River, nor with boat-building, before their talks with Parley Galloway. They would often hike into Jones Hole, carrying only fishing poles, some salt, and a few matches. They would then live off the land for a few days, and hike back out. One time, they decided to return to Vernal by way of the river, so they floated downstream holding onto cottonwood logs. When they came to rapids, they would let the logs go through, walk around, find the log below the rapid, and continue. They had also already built at least one skiff for seining, and later used it for fishing and hunting trips around Stewart Lake and Horseshoe Bend. As early as 1927, Bus described one such hunting trip in a letter to his brother Alt, then a student at Brigham Young University:

The boat sure works fine. It is twelve feet long and hauls three men across Green River at once, in a "high wind" too. Sunday we went down to Horse-shoe Bend. The bunch consisted of Frank Swain, Tom, Cap and myself. While we were across the river the wind came up and the waves on the river were sure rolling high. Cap, Frank, and myself got in the boat and crossed the river to the car. Frank got the short straw, and drew the job of rowing back across for Tom. By this time the wind was sure blowing like hell and the river was rolling high. We rowed that boat that day with paddles, Indian style, so [Frank] chose the best paddle and after a lot of coaxing and guying at him he got nerve enough to start. He put out to sea like Lindbergh starting across the Atlantic, but wait, the waves sure raised hell with that boat. He got two-thirds of the way across. A big wave hoisted the boat way up and [his] heart went up under his chin and shut off his wind. The next wave took the boat in the face and splashed water all over him. His courage and reason and everything else he might have had left him in a bunch. There is no retreat in history to equal the way old Frank pulled out. He ducked his head, socked the paddle into the water about six feet and the race was on. He paddled too much on one

side and went in a circle. When he was in the third round he broke the circle
and started back. I jerked out my Ingersoll [watch] but before I could shake it
and get it started he hit shore back on my side of the river. I never saw a boat
travel so darn fast in my life, it stood up on its hind end like the bronc old
Hessel rode hunting and how it did come. No one else ever made such speed
and I'm sure the record will stand 'til hell freezes over and they can't equal it
on skates either.

After they got through laughing at this display, they gave Frank a shot of
moonshine to revive him. Then Bus and Frank made another attempt, but the
waves were still too high.

> We took off our shoes and put them in the bottom of the boat. We then
> checked our life insurance and put to sea again. When we hit the center of
> the river the old boat raised up, slapped the water like a cannon going off
> and we put back for shore like a spirit out of hell. We made it back and yelled
> across at Tommy, told him he would have to stay there until the wind died
> down if it took six weeks.

"Pretty soon," Bus concluded, "the wind calmed down a bit and we crossed
and got him."

Fortified by this and similar experiences, and inspired by the long talks
with Parley, the cousins were eager to try the canyons. In their shop, Bus, Cap,
and the others built a boat. Based on sketches made by Parley Galloway, it was
sixteen feet long, with four feet of beam at the widest point. To withstand the
shock of hitting rocks, the bow was carved from a solid piece of oak. There
were two seats, so that the oarsman could row facing either direction, but
there were no watertight compartments. For supplies they took food in glass
canning jars; for life preservers, they had inner tubes cut down at a local gas
station so they would fit snugly under their arms. To repair the boat in case

of mishap, Bus brought along a bucket of tar, strips of canvas, carpet tacks, and tools. With their rifles, fishing poles, bedrolls, a couple of frying pans for cooking and bailing, and a sack of flour, they were ready to try the river.

Their first trip was in August 1931.[3] As in everything else they did together, Bus was the leader, and as he later noted, "appointed myself head boatman." Frank Swain, Tom Hatch, and Cap Mowrey were the passengers. Bay Hatch drove them up to Hideout Flat, on the Green below Flaming Gorge, and arranged to meet them below the mouth of Split Mountain Canyon in four days. From their first moment on the river, they realized that the elaborate and expensive oak bow was next to useless; most of the rocks they hit were with the side of the boat, not the bow. Nor had they fully learned Parley's lessons; that and inexperience proved to be their undoing. Their first day, as Bus told it, "There was one rapid, a small rock in the middle of it, and I managed to hit that, so I was one hundred percent right there."[4] Cap Mowrey later said that the rock knocked a hole in the side of the boat "big enough to throw a cat through."[5] But thinking fast, Cap clapped a pie tin over the hole and they were able to get to shore just as the boat sank. They repaired the hole with some strips of tin and tar, and continued on their way, a bit more carefully. Coming to Ashley Falls, they portaged that historic rapid, and ran Red Creek Rapid, just above Browns Park, only after careful scrutiny.

In Lodore Canyon, they portaged Disaster Falls, the first major rapid. They tried to run Hells Half Mile, the worst rapid in Lodore, but Bus lost control and capsized the boat, spilling not only them but all their supplies and gear into the river. The boat drifted down and lodged in the rocks at the bottom of the rapid. As struggled to reach shore, they could see their food supplies in glass jars floating along beside them. As each one hit a rock, there was a "pop." By the time they got to shore and righted the boat, they had nothing left to eat but a big onion and a couple of potatoes that Bus managed to grab. Bus and Cap landed on one side of the river, Tom and Frank on the other, sputtering and shivering. Even though neither one was a good swimmer, Bus and Frank made their way out to the boat and managed to free it from the rocks.

Also lost in the mishap, besides all their bedrolls and cooking gear, were their fishing poles. Fortunately, Frank Swain's old .30-40 Krag rifle was tied in and hadn't been lost. Spotting some mountain sheep looking on, he brought one down with a single shot, so onion and gamy, sandy mountain sheep meat was all they had to eat for the rest of the trip. Bus's feather pillow was another loss; he always said that he could sleep on a rock if he had a good pillow, and so had brought one from home. By the time they rescued it from the river, however, it took two of them just to drag it to shore. The pillow was left on a rock, another casualty of the spill.[6]

As they sat around a big campfire at Jones Hole, Bus munched on the onion, while the others gnawed on gritty mountain sheep meat. Naturally, the talk turned to river running. They decided that despite the mishaps, they wanted to explore the entire river, from the source, through the rugged lower canyons, to the Grand Canyon and beyond. They all had families and responsibilities— Bus had married Eva Caldwell in 1922, and already had three boys—but the lure of the canyons was still strong. They decided that when they could get time off from work and families, they would continue downriver and explore the stretch from Ouray to Green River, Utah. Then the next year they would try the dreaded Cataract Canyon to Lee's Ferry. After that, they would float the Grand Canyon, and who knows, even try the Amazon or the Yukon.

But first they had to get this trip over with. Two hard days on the river without any good food were beginning to tell; Cap noted that by the time they got to Island Park, "we's getting hungry enough to eat one another." There are nine miles of flat water to row to get through Island and Rainbow Parks, and they were so weak that they had to take turns rowing. The current is slow, and of course the wind was blowing upstream, as it always does in this stretch. No one was home at the Ruple ranch, so they could get no supplies there. In Split Mountain Canyon, they were beyond caring about how they navigated the many rapids, as long as they got through. By this time they had evolved a method for running rapids, whereby one of them stood in the stern and gave directions to the oarsman. This was the opposite of what Parley Galloway had told them, but it was faster, and that was what counted at this point. They finally reached the mouth of Split Mountain Canyon the last afternoon, and rowed down to Placer Point, where Eva and Frank Hatch were waiting with a big picnic lunch.

One realization to come out of the trip, besides the fact that glass jars were no good for carrying food, was that they needed better boats if they were going to attempt any more river explorations. While passing through Island Park, they had noticed something on the riverbank near the Ruple ranch that made them forget about their growling stomachs for a while. It was a boat, and what a boat! Decked over, with watertight compartments fore and aft, room for plenty of supplies and a couple of passengers. It was about eighteen feet long, and four and a half feet wide, with a flat bottom and enough rake, or rise between the center of the boat and the bow and stern to make it maneuverable in rapids. Bus's trained eye realized at once that this was a well-designed and well-made craft. How had old Hod Ruple come by such a sleek craft? The answer to that question involved none other than Parley Galloway.

In 1926, a couple of dudes from back east named Todd and Page decided to spend their vacation floating the canyons of the Green River. For a guide, they hired a man from Green River, Utah, named H. Elwyn Blake. Blake had been a boatman for the 1922 U.S. Geological Survey damsite investigation of the upper Green, and other government surveys, and was an experienced riverman. The survey had used custom-built Galloway-style boats, by now the standard on the river. Todd and Page bought two of them and had Blake and a local man from Green River, Wyoming, Curley Hale, recaulk and refurbish them. Starting from Green River, Wyoming, in August, 1926, they had an exciting but successful trip down the river until their last day in Lodore. Below all the rapids, one of the boats was pinned immovably on a midstream rock, forcing them to abandon that one and finish the trip in their remaining boat.[7] The next year, Parley Galloway and Frank Gerber were trapping down Lodore, when they found the abandoned boat. Freeing it from the rocks, Galloway took it down to Island Park and sold it to Hod Ruple, who used it for herding his cattle back and forth across the river. It was this boat that Bus and the others saw in Island Park.

Bus later came back and made measurements from the boat, and as soon as he had time back home, set about building his own version. First, he reduced the length to fifteen and a half feet—he felt that eighteen was too long for the width. For watertight compartments, Bus used carbide cans built into the decks. These cans, which contained the carbide that miners used in their headlamps, had a screw-down lid with a gasket. Not only would they keep supplies and gear dry, they would provide extra flotation. Bus lavished extra care on the boat, making sure it would hold up under the beating that any boat gets running the rocky canyons. In October 1931, Bus, Alt, Tom and a friend of Tom's named Chuck Henderson tried the new craft out with a run through Split Mountain. It worked perfectly, so Bus and Cap built another just like it. In a bit of whimsy, they named the two boats the *What Next?* and the *Don't Know*.[8] Now they were ready to make good on their pledge to explore the rest of the river.

Meanwhile, Frank Swain had moved to Bingham, Utah, in 1930 to take a job as security officer for Utah Copper Company. There he got to know the company doctor, Russell Frazier, who fancied himself an outdoorsman. Frank told Frazier wonderful stories about the hunting and fishing out in Vernal. Frazier wanted to take a trip to the Uinta Basin and try his luck, so Frank

contacted his cousin Bus and arranged to take Frazier and another Bingham man, Bill Fahrni, on a fishing trip to Jones Hole in the summer of 1932. Camped by the Green River, the two cousins regaled Frazier and Fahrni with tales of running the river. Being an adventurous sort, Frazier asked to be taken down through Lodore. When he offered to pay for supplies and transportation, Bus and Frank agreed. This time the crew would consist of Bus and Frank as boatmen, with Tom Hatch, Dr. Frazier, Bill Fahrni, and two other Salt Lake men, Rhinehard van Evers and Dr. Henderson, as passengers. They started from Hideout Flats the following September, and had clear sailing for the first four days; but in Lodore, they learned that the river was still in command.

> On Thursday as they were going through Ladore, the most hazardous canyon of the entire trip, they had the misfortune to lose one boat with all its equipment and provisions. Riding over Disaster Falls, where Captain Ashley's crew of seven men lost their lives by drowning in his famous expedition through the canyon, [sic] the boat passed over in safety but struck a huge boulder at the foot of the falls, turning the boat over and throwing it under 4 feet of water. Here it was held by the suction of the current.[9]

Shaken by this experience, they lined the other boat down the left side of the rapid and then tried to salvage part of the supplies. But the current was too

Riverman

swift and the boat pinned too securely, and they had to give up the attempt after a day and a half. As the *Vernal Express* breathlessly noted,

> The sinking and abandoning of the one boat at Disaster Falls represented a loss of more than $500 to the party. Often the boats would ride in rapids more than 30 miles per hour. Where the canyon walls suddenly narrowed and the racing river was confined to a narrow gorge, the sudden change would cause the water at the edge of the stream to raise into [the] air 10 to 15 feet and form a huge trough.

Nor were their troubles behind them. In Split Mountain, the boat capsized, pinning Frank Swain and Dr. Frazier underneath. As Frank struggled to get free, he kicked Frazier in the head with his hobnailed boots, knocking him unconscious. But they soon revived him, and finished out the journey without any more mishaps. When they landed at Jensen, the bottom of the boat showed hard use, and they had to bail constantly to keep it from sinking. The *Vernal Express* article about their trip concluded optimistically, however, noting that they were already planning another trip from Jensen to Lee's Ferry the next year. Despite their bad experiences, they weren't through with the river yet. Nor was the river through with them.

Before they could plan any more trips, though, there was a lot of work to be done. First order of business was to salvage the *What Next?*, still pinned in Disaster Falls. In November, when the water was much lower, Bus, Frank, Cap, and Garn Swain took the *Don't Know* and floated down to the site of the wreck. There they found the boat intact, despite being pinned in the river for two months. Bus had brought 150 feet of steel cable, chains, and two block and tackles; with this equipment, they soon had the boat freed. They recovered all of their gear intact, except for the wool blankets, which had shrunk to the size of saddle blankets. But all the boat needed was some minor repairs—a testament to how well-built the boat was in the first place—and it was ready to be taken down through the rest of the canyon. They rowed both boats out to the mouth of Split Mountain the next day, where they were loaded onto trucks and taken back to Vernal.

Next they needed more boats. Alt Hatch wanted to go along on the next leg of the river journey, and offered to buy the materials for a boat if Bus and Cap would build it. It was similar to the *What Next?* and the *Don't Know* in all but one respect. There were no carbide cans available for watertight compartments, so Bus had a local welder construct tin boxes that were then

Canyon of Lodore, 1932

Left to right: Bus Hatch, Dr. Frazier, Rhinehard Van Evers, Frank Swain, Bill Fahrni, Dr. Henderson

built into the bow and stern of the boat. These had a lid with a gasket that could be tightened down with thumbscrews. Since Alt had financed the boat, they named it for his daughter, calling it the *Lota Ve*. Despite being kicked in the head—or perhaps because of it—Dr. Frazier was anxious to go with them on the next leg of the river voyage. He and Bill Fahrni offered to finance yet another boat, which Bus and Cap built that winter. Except for minor details, it was identical to the *Lota Ve*.[10] Now they were ready for their greatest challenge yet: Cataract Canyon.

Before tackling Cataract Canyon, though, they decided to float the rest of the way down the Green River, through Desolation, Gray, Labyrinth, and Stillwater Canyons. The crew for the first leg of this journey consisted of Bus, Frank, Alt, Dr. Frazier and Bill Fahrni. They started from Ouray, a little town on the Ute Indian Reservation about fifty miles down river from Jensen, on July 24, 1933. They used the *Lota Ve* and Dr. Frazier's new boat. This time they took along a small outboard motor to speed them through the miles of flat water. Desolation and Gray Canyons, with their moderate rapids and swift current, gave no trouble to the by-now experienced river runners, and they reached Green River, Utah, about five days later. There Alt, whose vacation was over, left the party and was replaced by Cap and Tom Hatch.

Camped near the railroad bridge, Dr Frazier was reluctant to leave the shade of the cottonwood trees, so he gave Bus and Frank $20 and sent them into town to buy supplies for the next leg of the journey. It was about a mile

Riverman

into the little town, and they were hot and dry. The first building they passed was a saloon, so Bus suggested that they go in and get the really essential supplies—beer—before continuing with their mission. The bartender made them take off their hobnailed boots, and then they went inside. Frank asked the bartender how much beer he had. "Four dozen bottles," was the reply. "Got a sack? Then fill her up."

Fortified, and with only ten dollars left, they continued on into town. Passing a hardware store, they decided they could hunt for game to fill out the larder, if they had a gun. So they bought a .22 single-shot rifle for $6.50 and spent the rest for ammunition, and headed back to the boats. On the way back, they met the local Mormon bishop. He asked them their business, and when he found out they were headed down into Cataract Canyon, he gave them a big sack of string beans, some cantaloupes and watermelons, and said a prayer for their safety. Dr. Frazier was none too pleased with the results of their shopping trip; Bus's only reply was to say he should've gone himself if he didn't like it.

They used their motor to get through Labyrinth and Stillwater Canyons, and reached the confluence of the Green and the Colorado about the first of August. Cataract Canyon, then known as the "Graveyard of the Colorado," lived up to its fearsome reputation. Before Lake Powell covered the worst of its rapids in the 1960s, Cataract had over forty miles of tumultuous rapids, including Dark Canyon rapid, considered to be one of the most difficult on the Colorado. Realizing that if they lost their boats there, it was an impossibly long walk across the desert back to civilization, they were for once more cautious. Most of the worst rapids they lined their boats around, an arduous procedure under the best of conditions. And it was hardly that; the water was thick with mud, and it was blisteringly hot. In the middle of the canyon, they were caught by a sudden rise in the river and had to spend the night pulling their boats up away from the rising water. When they did decide to run a rapid, the muddy water made it doubly difficult, as an article in the *Vernal Express* described.

> Many of their most thrilling experiences were had while riding waves from fifteen to thirty feet high, with a speed of thirty or more miles per hour. For more than one day they rode waves of mud which would hold up great cakes of clay, every minute of which seemed as though it might be their last. In this there was so much stress they forgot to take a movie of their flight. One boat was capsized and the only loss sustained was a bucket they used to bail out water with. Water was so heavy with mud and the waves so high that some of the men were knocked almost senseless by the impact as the boat sped over the crest. After leaving the crest the boat at times would be thrown into the air and only kept upright by swaying from side to side.[11]

Another time, the article noted, Bus stepped out of the boat into what appeared to be a puddle, and "immediately was plunged over his head. When he shot out [the] others could not help him without endangering the lives of the remainder of the party." One can't help but suspect that they were laughing too hard to help him anyway.

Just below Dark Canyon Rapid, they stopped long enough for Bus to affix a copper plaque he had made, bearing their names and the date.[12] They pushed on, hurrying because of the heat and their scanty supplies. They saw no one for the entire ten days it took them to get through Cataract, nor did they see any game. They had been shooting at the few geese they saw, but couldn't hit anything, so they were short of food. At the head of Glen Canyon, they found a placer mining camp just below Hite. No one was home at the camp, but they found canned goods, flour, and other supplies in a tent. The men gathered up some food and left a note explaining what had happened.[13] They were ready to leave when Dr. Frazier spied a gasoline stove, and decided that they would have hot food that day. The others said they knew nothing about operating such a contraption, but Dr. Frazier insisted that he knew all about them. He pumped the stove up and lit it; burning gasoline squirted out of the stove, set the tent on fire and almost burned down the entire camp.

Even though they were hot, thirsty, and short of supplies, they found time to see some of the sights in Glen Canyon as they floated through on the last leg of their voyage. They stopped at Music Temple, and saw the inscriptions left by the Powell parties sixty years before, and at Hole in the Rock, where Mormon pioneers had carved a passage out of the cliffs to get their wagons across the

Riverman

river. At Dr. Frazier's urging, they searched unsuccessfully for the Crossing of the Fathers, where Dominguez and Escalante had crossed the river in 1776.[14] Finally, they took the seven-mile hike up Forbidding Canyon to see Rainbow Bridge, one of the wonders of the canyon country. They reached Lee's Ferry the middle of August, and stored the boats at the USGS gauging station there, for the next years' planned run of the Grand Canyon. Mrs. Frazier met them and took everyone back to Bingham in their Cadillac.

Bus had come a long way since the first trip down the Green a scant two years before. From open boats, clumsily run, he had progressed to sleek, state-of-the-art craft, and now possessed considerable skill at the oars of a river boat. Bus was never wedded to any particular technique, Galloway or otherwise. He used whichever way worked best at the time, and he was successful at it. As an article about their Cataract Canyon trip noted, Bus and the others had more than a thousand river miles to their credit, without any major mishaps. On all of these trips, Bus had been the unspoken leader. His boat ran first in the rapids, and he often ran all the boats through by himself. He was first to help with lining or portaging, or with cooking and other duties around camp.

They had had their share of hardships and mishaps, yet through it all—the capsizes and the pinned boat in Lodore, the hot, hungry trip through Cataract—Bus maintained his sense of humor. When they did capsize a boat, or pin one on a rock, it was no big thing. They were on the river to have a good time, and no little inconvenience was going to interfere with that. For their next adventures, the Grand Canyon, and the wild, unexplored Salmon River of Idaho, Bus would need all of his nerve and his sense of humor.

endnotes

1 Frank Swain interview, 2 March 1984. The story of Parley Galloway and how Bus learned to build boats is also told in *The Middle Fork and the Sheepeater War*, by Johnny Carrey and Cort Conley (Backeddy Books, 1977).

2 Parley Galloway died of exposure and starvation just a few years later near Panguitch, Utah. He is buried in the Panguitch cemetery.

3 "Perilous Boat Trip Made by Vernal Party," *Vernal Express*, 27 August 1931.

4 Bus Hatch interview with Fred Washburn, ca. 1964. Mr. Washburn, a friend of Bus, invited Bus to dinner and recorded their conversation on a reel-to-reel tape recorder. When I was writing this book, Mr. Washburn kindly offered me a copy of the tape, which provided insights into Bus's character that I would otherwise never have had, and allowed me to hear some of the stories in Bus's own voice. This was invaluable, and even though Mr. Washburn has since passed on, I remain grateful to him for this kindness. Hereafter referred to as the "Bus Hatch interview."

5 Royce "Cap" Mowrey interview by Royce Hatch, 1976. Hereafter referred to as "Mowrey interview." Like the 1964 Bus Hatch interview, this proved to be a very valuable primary source. The tape was supplied by the Hatch family.

6 To this day, Hatch River Expeditions includes a nice pillow in their rental sleeping outfits, a legacy of Bus's love of a good pillow.

7 The story of the Todd-Page party, as well as Blake's other river experiences, is well told in *Rough-water man: Elwyn Blake's Colorado River expeditions*, by Richard E. Westwood. (University of Nevada Press, 1992). The rock that they wrecked their boat on is just below Rippling Brook camp, and known to some as "Og's Rock," after "Og" West, the member of the party who was rowing the boat when it was wrecked.

8 In another bit of whimsy, Bus also added the phrase *Who Cares?* to the other side of the bow of the *Don't Know*. In a film made of the 1932 trip, it appears that there were three boats instead of two; but if you look closely at one point, you can see both names on the bow of the boat.

9 "Thrilling Boat Trip Down Green River," *Vernal Express*, 15 September 1932. p. 1. "Ladore" is the common but incorrect spelling of the canyon, and you still see it today. The tale about the loss of seven of Captain Ashley's men is another local legend; Ashley lost no boats nor men on his 1825 Green River trip. John Wesley Powell lost a boat in Disaster Falls in 1869, but no men.

10 Frazier's boat went by several names during its river career, being known variously as the *Swallow,* the *Helldiver*, and the *Colorado.*

11 "Vernal Men Successfully Navigate Colorado River Canyon," *Vernal Express*, 17 August 1933. p. 1

12 The spot where they left the plaque had already become a "river register," where river parties such as Clyde Eddy left their names. The register, and the plaque, were covered by the waters of Lake Powell in the 1960s.

13 While this might seem like common thievery, it was an accepted practice at the time, part of the "code of the West." If you needed supplies you took them, and someday, if someone else needed supplies, you gave them away.

14 Frazier finally located the Crossing in 1940, and marked it with a plaque. It too was covered up by Lake Powell in the 1960s.

The Dusty Dozen

WHEN Bus and his companions pushed off from Lee's Ferry in July, 1934, for their voyage down the Grand Canyon, less than fifty men had preceded them.[1] The Canyon was in many ways still the "Great Unknown" that John Wesley Powell had explored less than a hundred years earlier. Powell's exploratory voyages in 1869 and 1871–2 had been filled with privation and toil, and the first had turned into a race for survival at the end. Three of Powell's men had hiked out of the canyon in 1869, only to disappear into the desert, never to be seen again.[2] The next party to attempt the Canyon, the Brown-Stanton Expedition of 1889, lost three men before they had gone 25 miles. Since then a few other parties had made the journey, but all had met with hardship and danger—as recently as 1928, Glen and Bessie Hyde, the "Honeymoon Couple," had been lost in the lower canyon. Clearly the cousins and their passengers were in for a rough time.

But Bus and his companions were well prepared and felt themselves seasoned by their previous experiences on the upper river. Alt Hatch would be a boatman on this trip, and Bus and Cap had taken him on a training trip down the Yampa River in the spring of 1934. There, Alt had rowed his new boat, the *Lota Ve*, and they were also accompanied by Dr. Wallace Calder, a Vernal physician. They started from Lily Park, Colorado, the first week of June. The Yampa was at flood, so it only took them three days to run all the way to Jensen, Utah. The Yampa Canyon in June is a beautiful place, full of freshly-leafed-out box elder trees and hundreds of geese. Bus and the others saw mountain lion, bear, and elk tracks; deer were plentiful. Most importantly, Alt got the feel of handling a boat in fast water.[3]

The next month they took another trip to get in shape for the Grand Canyon adventure, scheduled to start the end of July. This trip had another purpose as well: Bus and Frank took Earl Clyde and Lee Kay, Utah state game wardens, down the river to look for beaver, which had just about been trapped out along the Green. Bill Fahrni was also along for the ride. They started from Hideout Flat and floated to Jensen, but the trip turned out to be more of an adventure than they bargained for, as an article about the trip noted:

> Although frequently capsized during the voyage, and soaked to the skin from morning till night while running the rapids, there was only one serious mishap, so skillfully did the veteran river runners Bus Hatch, Frank Swain, and Bill Fahrni manipulate the watertight 16-foot craft. That one mishap almost cost the life of Fahrni, however, quick work by Hatch averted the catastrophe when their boat crashed, hanging momentarily on a rock before the entrance to Lower Disaster Falls, where the entire river enters a subterranean channel beneath a ledge. Hatch managed to jump ashore as Fahrni was catapulted into the stream, Hatch grabbed the life line on one end of the boat, and Fahrni clung to the other, subsequently being pulled to safety.[4]

Nor were Bill Fahrni's troubles over. Camped at Jones Hole, Fahrni was bitten on the heel by a rattlesnake which had crawled into his bedroll. His foot immediately began to swell, but unfortunately for him, Dr. Frazier wasn't on the trip. So they resorted to a home remedy, plying him with whiskey and putting his foot into a bucket of water, while Bus rowed him out the rest of the way to Jensen. There he was put in a car and rushed to the Vernal hospital. By then the crisis seemed to have passed, but Fahrni had to spend a couple of weeks in the hospital in Salt Lake City anyway. As he later commented, the whiskey and water treatment was effective, and he was fine until the doctors got to him.

Fahrni's experience looked like a bad omen for their Grand Canyon trip, but Frazier, at least, was confident. In an interview, he dismissed a statement that the "Colorado River Club," as he called the group of river runners, should have a different name:

> Someone has remarked that we ought to call it the suicide club, but we feel different. All of the party have had plenty of experience in rapid water. We

Riverman

have good boats well made. Bus Hatch and Royce Mowrey are the builders and can rebuild them at any point on the river from a drift pile. Our party includes a doctor and Frank Swain, Vernal's leading undertaker. All we lack is a preacher, and Frank thinks he can do that in a pinch.

Frazier concluded the interview with a jaunty jingle:

There's no greater thrill,
Than the chance of a spill
In a rapid that's angrily white,
But the one that you feel,
When the leveling keel,
Proclaims that your boat's still upright.[5]

For the Grand Canyon the "Colorado River Club" would use four boats: the *Lota Ve* and Dr. Frazier's boat, stored at Lee's Ferry since the end of their Cataract Canyon voyage the previous year, and their two older boats, the *What Next?* and the *Don't Know*. These latter two Bus, Alt, Frank Swain, and Cap Mowrey brought down from Vernal in Bus's truck a week before they were scheduled to launch. All the boats were in poor condition from storage, and needed to be recaulked and repaired to get them into shape for the difficult days ahead.

After a couple of days, the rest of the party showed up. Dr. Frazier and Bill Fahrni had waited in Salt Lake City for the last two members of the crew, Clyde Eddy—who had run the Canyon in 1927—and a newsreel photographer from Wilkes-Barre, Pennsylvania, Fred Jayne. Eddy, seeking to make a profit from movies of the trip, brought Jayne along as the cameraman. Jayne showed up wearing a golf suit, with knickers covered with a large check pattern; Eddy was wearing a light gray suit. The cousins, who by this point "looked like a bunch of mud hens," looked at each other in disbelief. "Fred," Bus said, "Have you got any other clothes?" "I didn't figure to go down the Canyon in these," Jayne replied. In truth, Jayne was no dude. He was an experienced and well-known newsreel photographer, and had once hung by his heels from an airplane at 10,000 feet to make a film.

They launched from Lee's Ferry at 10 A.M. on July 19, 1934. Bus and Fred Jayne were in the lead boat—Jayne had looked at Bus and said, "This man is about my size. I'm going to ride with him." Frank Swain was next, with Clyde Eddy in one of the open boats, followed by Alt and Cap in the *Lota Ve*; Dr.

Frazier and Bill Fahrni brought up the rear in the Doctor's boat. The water was low, for these were the dust bowl years. The Colorado was running less than 1800 cfs, barely enough to float a boat. Between Lee's Ferry and Badger Creek, the first significant rapid, were three rapids that don't even show up in a normal water year. Badger was a nest of rocks, "impossible to run," so they lined it on the left side. Soap Creek, just above where Frank Mason Brown drowned in July 1889, and the scene of many mishaps, was no better. "It could have been run," Alt Hatch wrote in his diary, "by chancing life and boats, but after talking with [the] group we decided to line it."[6] While lining Soap Creek, Bill Fahrni—his bad luck still with him—broke his hand and had to suffer the rest of the trip, so Dr. Frazier took over the boat.

On they went, deeper and deeper into Marble Canyon. They ran an occasional rapid, but more often lined their boats along the side of the river. In House Rock Rapid, about mile 17, Jayne had occasion to regret his decision to ride with Bus. As Bus later described it, "I gave Jayne a nice ride in House Rock. Two boats tipped over there. We struck a log and tipped over slick. Below it was a smooth pool. Jayne came up with his hat hanging around his neck and his Bell & Howell camera around his wrist."[7]

Bus held onto the boat, while Jayne, holding on to his cumbersome camera, was swept around in the eddy below. When the others yelled to Bus that Jayne

was struggling to stay afloat, Bus shouted "son of a bitch, if he can't swim, he can drown!" There was no danger—the eddy was a "millpond," according to Bus—but Jayne came up a changed man. He sat down and began to clean and dry his camera, not saying much, but it was evident that the spill had terrified him.

Because of incidents like this, Dr. Frazier and Clyde Eddy insisted that they line the rapids, a cumbersome and arduous process whereby the boats were let down along the shore by means of ropes attached at the bow and stern of the boat. When they came to the "Roaring Twenties," a series of rapids in close succession, Bus and Cap began to grumble—this lining was hot work, Bus said, and they had only made four miles the first day. When Dr. Frazier and Eddy said that lining was necessary for the "safety of the expedition," Bus replied hotly, "Hell! I didn't come down here to run this canyon on my feet!" Soon after, one of the boats got away from them while it was being lined and became pinned on a rock. Bus and Cap waded out into the river, held a piece of canvas so that it diverted the flow, and freed the boat. A little while later, when they stopped to scout a rapid, Bus took Cap aside. "Are you with me?" he asked. "Let's run these rapids. If they want to line their boats, they can line them. You get in with me and we'll run 'em. To hell with lining 'em." [8] Before the others were aware of what was happening, Bus and Cap were bouncing through the tailwaves. After that, there was no more talk of lining "for the safety of the expedition."

At Vasey's Paradise, a complex of freshwater springs about mile 32, they stopped to enjoy the cool, clear water. Just upstream are several large caves, and they climbed up to see if there was anything in them. Alt, Cap, and Dr. Frazier dug in one cave, while Bus explored another. Cap Mowrey made a gruesome find: a skeleton of a man, with "coarse, black hair," still dressed in buckskins, and with both legs broken. There were other strange signs: when they dug under the body, a "bad odor" rose from the ground, and the chest of the skeleton was covered with ashes from where someone had built a fire of yucca leaves. No answers were found to these riddles, and the skeleton gradually disappeared as tourists took home grisly souvenirs of their Grand Canyon adventures.[9]

Bus, in the meanwhile, had found something of much greater importance than the remains of some unfortunate prospector. Digging in a nearby cave, he unearthed a number of small figurines. These were willow twigs, split lengthwise and intricately bent and wrapped to resemble deer or perhaps bighorn sheep. Toys, he thought, and brought home about two dozen of them in a paper sack for his young son Don to play with. Later, word of the figurines got out. Bus was contacted by the American Museum of Natural History about his find, asking if he would donate them to the museum. When they were examined by radiocarbon dating, they were found to be over 3,000 years old, the oldest evidence of man in the Grand Canyon.

On July 24, they came to Hance Rapid, the first truly difficult rapid in the Canyon. Hance is a tricky rapid even at optimum water conditions, a nest of boulders beset with holes. At the low water the "Dusty Dozen" (for by now they were so styling themselves) had a terrible time. The upper end of the rapid was literally dammed off by boulders, and Bus and Cap notwithstanding, they were forced to rope the boats down. Immediately after Hance, the river enters the Upper Granite Gorge, a narrow, gloomy section of the canyon lined with black Vishnu Schist, a metamorphosed granite. The walls come right down to the river; they couldn't have lined the fierce rapids in the gorge if they had wanted to. Although there are rapids every mile in the upper gorge, the next difficult one was Sockdolager, which they ran successfully. Then they came to Grapevine. As they drifted into the head of the rapid, Dr. Frazier and Bill Fahrni got to arguing about the proper course to take, and ran their boat up onto a rock. Frank, seeing what was happening, steered his boat close to the rock, and Bill Fahrni jumped into his boat, landing in Frank's lap. Laughing

at these antics, Alt and Cap ran into Bus's boat, which was next in line. Only Frank managed to run the rapid safely. Cap Mowrey walked back upriver with a rope tied to his waist, jumped into the river, and swam to the stranded boat. They then attached pulleys to the boat and pulled it free. After Grapevine, Doc Frazier had had enough of running rapids. He still rowed his boat in the flat stretches, but had Bus run it through the remaining rapids.

The next day they came to the Bright Angel Trail. Time for a break, they reasoned, so they decided they would tie up their boats and climb out to the South Rim. There was another reason for climbing out: Fred Jayne had had enough. Hanging by your heels from an airplane was one thing; running rapids every day with a "wildcat" like Bus Hatch was another, and he had decided to quit the expedition. Besides all of Jayne's camera equipment, film, and baggage, they decided to carry out the outboard motor they had hoped to use at the lower end of the canyon. During one of their mishaps, they had been unloading a boat to free it from the rocks, and someone had dropped the magneto for the motor into the river. Without it the motor was useless dead weight. So Bus, Alt, Frank, and Cap shouldered heavy packs and started up the trail, followed by the others, who carried nothing.

It is eight miles to the south rim from the river, with an elevation gain of almost 5,000 feet. Within the first couple of miles, they passed a fountain by the side of the trail. Figuring that there were such stations all the way up, they

Lining Horn Creek Rapid.

Bus in boat; Frazier in river next to it.

Caption reads:

To Bus Hatch, without equal in the tough places. With warm personal regards, Clyde Eddy

decided to cache all their water to save the extra weight. It turned out to be a serious mistake, as there was no more water until they reached the rim. They climbed and climbed, and the day grew hotter and hotter. Dr. Frazier and Clyde Eddy were the first to drop out, collapsing by the side of the trail. They were soon joined by Jayne and Bill Fahrni, gasping in the heat. Bus and the rest struggled on, their tongues swelling as they trudged toward the distant rim. Finally only Bus, Frank, and Cap were left, and they staggered into the El Tovar Hotel, crying for water. By this time it was night, and the cool air and the water soon revived them. Dropping their loads, they took a bucket filled with coffee and sugar and walked back down the trail to rescue the others. They found Alt, and gave him some of the coffee—he revived and started up. Next they came on Fred Jayne, crawling along the trail, his knees bloody. Finally, halfway down the trail, were Dr. Frazier and Clyde Eddy. After a few deep draughts of the sweet coffee, they had regained enough strength to make it to the top.

The next day, they did justice to a huge breakfast at the El Tovar, and went over to Emery Kolb's studio to meet that famous river runner. Kolb had had his photography studio on the south Rim since 1902, and had with his brother Ellsworth run the Colorado in Galloway-style wooden boats in 1911. Bus and

Knocking down the dust at riverside waterfall, mile 156.

Left to right:

Cap Mowrey, Clyde Eddy, Bill Fahrni, Alt Hatch, Bus Hatch, Frank Swain

the others visited with Emery, and then sat in on his daily lecture and showing of the movie made during the 1911 trip. After it was over, Emery introduced the party and made them all stand up before the crowd of tourists. They decided to stay over that night and rest up, before heading back into the canyon the next day.

Rested and much refreshed by their visit to the South Rim, they were back on the river on July 27. They did not, however, get off to a good start, as Alt noted in his diary:

> July 27. Left Bright Angel at 10:30. Just got out of camp and going over a rapid I hit a rock and Cap went out. Went a little farther and Frank tipped over in Granite Falls. In Hermit Rapids Bus broke an oar and landed on a rock. Doc and Bill got pin[n]ed on a rock by the time we got off it was time to camp.[10]

But better days were ahead. By now they were hardened to the heat and the labor, and their rapid running skills were honed to a fine point. Below Bright Angel there are over fifty difficult rapids, and even more at the low water level they were running on, and yet they ran almost all of them. Only at the worst ones, such as Dubendorff and Upset, were they forced to resort to lining. Had there been enough water, they no doubt would have run them as well. Dr. Frazier and Clyde Eddy were still worried about the "safety of the expedition," but by this point had given up trying to dissuade Bus and the others from running the rapids. Eddy in particular didn't like running rapids; Frank Swain later recalled that "Eddy was so frightened he got down in the bottom just like a wet hound." However, Frank went on to admit, "I was scairt too." But it was too hot to line the boats, and they were getting tired of the river and, one suspects, of each other.

By the time they were approaching Lava Falls, the faithful *Don't Know*, which Frank had been rowing, was worn out, and he had to bail constantly just to keep it afloat. Over Frazier's and Eddy's objections, they decided to abandon it and go on in the remaining three. Frank switched over to Dr. Frazier's boat, and Frazier was from this point a passenger. Frazier and Cap were the only ones of the party who smoked; Frazier kept his tobacco and papers sealed in honey cans. Nervous about the rapids, he was constantly asking Frank Swain to open the compartment on his boat so he could have a smoke. This began to get on Frank's nerves, and he finally asked Frazier when he was going to quit. "Tomorrow," Frazier would reply, "I'll quit tomorrow." Finally, Frank was fed up. Frazier asked him to get out his cigarettes one more time, and Frank did as he asked, undoing the thumbscrews and opening the hatch. "Now when are you going to quit, Doc?" "Tomorrow. Hush, I'll quit tomorrow." Frank opened the tin, looked at Frazier, and tossed the contents into the river. "I guess you will." "Why you mean son-of-a-bitch," Frazier said. "What did you call me?" asked Frank. When Frazier repeated it, Frank punched him in the mouth, loosening Frazier's front two teeth. Frank immediately felt sorry he had done it, and offered to tighten them up for him. "I've buried men with teeth that were looser than those," he offered helpfully—besides being deputy sheriff Frank was also the undertaker in Vernal. But the teeth never did tighten, and Frazier finally had to get a bridge.

The next day they came to Lava Falls. This is the premier rapid in the Grand Canyon, with a steep drop, violent waves and holes, and a fearsome reputation. They could hear the roar of the rapid almost a mile upstream. Most early river parties (and some later ones) lined Lava Falls, but it just too hot and they were too tired, so they decided to run it. Dr. Frazier decided that he would ride with Bus, having had enough of Frank for a little while. "Fine with me," said Bus; "tack down your hat and let's go." Bus put his boat right down the middle of Lava's tumultuous waves, and Frazier was "thrown fair and square."

When the boat rolled over, he went over the side with a chew of tobacco in his mouth, a frying pan (used for bailing) in one hand and his camera in the other. When he came up the first time, he had swallowed the chew, and had only the frying pan. He went under again, and when he came up, even the frying pan was gone. By this time Bus had already righted the boat and was bailing the water out with a tin can. Frazier swam to the side of the boat and started to climb in. "Goddamn you," Bus yelled, "if you try to climb up that side [thereby flipping the boat] I'll hit you with this oar. Hold onto the back." Below the rapid, Bus helped him back in, but Frazier too had had enough of Bus's quick temper, and after that, Bus rode alone. Frazier rode with Frank and Clyde Eddy the rest of the trip. After this mishap, they lined the other boats through the rapid.

On August 3, they reached Separation Rapid, where O.G. Howland, Seneca Howland, and Bill Dunn, three of John Wesley Powell's crew, had left the river on August 28, 1869. They climbed out to the North Rim, only to be killed by Shivwits Indians for some imagined wrong. When the monument to Powell was dedicated on the south rim in 1916, certain individuals[11] had caused the Howlands and Dunn to be left off the list of crew members, on the specious grounds that they had "deserted" the Major. Frazier, to his credit, saw this as a wrong, and had decided to do something about it. In Salt Lake, he'd had a bronze plaque made, which read:

IN MEMORY OF
SENECA HOWLAND
O.G. HOWLAND
WM. H. DUNN
WHO LEFT THE FIRST POWELL PARTY AT
THIS POINT AUG. 28, 1869 & WERE KILLED
BY INDIANS ON THE SHIVWITS PLATEAU.
ERECTED BY
COLORADO RIVER CLUB
1934

They had carried the plaque all the way down the river. Now Bus and Cap drilled holes in the rock above Separation Rapid and, "with appropriate ceremony," bolted the plaque to the canyon wall. Below it, they fixed a smaller copper plaque listing the date and their names, which Bus had made using a punch. Pictures were taken to record the event, Frazier and Clyde Eddy walked around the rapid while the others ran the boats through, and they camped on the beach below. The ghosts of the Howlands and Bill Dunn had finally seen justice done.[12]

The last leg of the trip was a "nightmare," in Bus's words. The heat was incredible, often reaching 120 degrees during the day. They tried fishing for channel catfish, but since they were so low on food they didn't want to waste any on bait. Frank tried using the little whiptail lizards for bait, but they were difficult to catch, so it hardly seemed worth the effort, even though the catfish loved them. They were down to their last cans of food, the labels of which had long since washed off, so that each night's meal was a surprise—but more often than not it was, once again, pork and beans.[13] All they had to drink was black tea, made with the muddy river water. There were still many fierce rapids to be passed, including one of the worst on the river, Lava Cliff. Frazier, Eddy, and Bill Fahrni took one look and decided to walk around, and Bus rowed them across the river and dropped them off. The others ran the boats through, but not without difficulty. Frank Swain hit the cliff on the right and capsized. The water was so turbulent it was like "bromo-seltzer," and he could hardly keep afloat. Finally, he grabbed the trailing bowline of the boat and was able to pull himself onto the bottom of the boat. At the bottom of the rapid they righted the boat, picked up the others, and went on. They could do little else by this point.

Finally, on August 7, nineteen days out of Lee's Ferry, they rounded a corner and there was the still-incomplete Boulder Dam. The massive diversion

Riverman

The plaque at Separation Rapid. Left to right: Alt Hatch, Cap Mowrey, Bus Hatch, Bill Fahrni, Dr. Frazier

tunnels had been completed, and the Colorado turned out of its ancient bed. Bus and Frank tried to convince the engineer in charge to let them run the river through the tunnel, but he refused. It was just as well; their boats were all but worn out, and they were just about used up. Dr. Frazier borrowed $7.50 from Frank, all the money any of them had, to get a bus ticket back to Salt Lake City for Clyde Eddy. After Eddy, Frazier, and Fahrni left, the others were left to wait for the Doctor to bring back his car from Las Vegas. Right across the road was a saloon for the construction workers. It was sheer torture, they all remembered, to sit across from that saloon with no money. Then they noticed a man admiring their boats, still tied up in the river. It turned out he was the saloon keeper, and he wanted a boat in the worst way. Then and there they worked out a deal. They would trade him the *What Next?* for all the beer they could drink until Frazier returned. They shook hands all around, and retired to the cool saloon and the cold beer. Never was there a better trade, they agreed, as they lifted cold bottles of beer to toast the river and the canyon.

The "Dusty Dozen" had floated over three hundred miles of river, and run over two hundred rapids. They had done it under conditions of heat and low water never before (and not often since) faced by river runners. Before them, less than fifty men had made the trip and lived; after them would come the deluge. Now more people than that leave Lee's Ferry for a trip through the canyon in a single day. An article in the *Vernal Express*, appropriately titled "River Trip to Boulder Dam Hazardous," noted:

[F]our Vernal men returned last week, feeling mighty fortunate to get back home alive. All of the venturesome rivermen received enough thrills to last their lifetime and none are seeking to again risk their lives for the thrills they might receive.

Not quite true, for they were already planning their next adventure. This time, however, they turned their attention to the north, and set their sights on Idaho's Middle Fork of the Salmon, then on down the main Salmon—the River of No Return. It was Frazier's idea to run the Middle Fork. He had heard about the river from a hunting guide he had met, Austin Lightfoot. Lightfoot's tales of the clearwater Salmon, with trees coming down to the river and holes full of salmon and trout, intrigued Frazier. When Lightfoot told him that only one other party had ever made it down the river, Frazier determined to give it a try. Despite his experiences in the Grand Canyon, Frazier had lost none of his exploring urges. First he told Frank Swain about it. "I'll try that Salmon," said the Doctor. "You may handle the river, but can you handle Hatch?" Frank replied. Frazier felt that he could, and he and Frank soon had Bus and Cap convinced; Alt and Bill Fahrni would accompany them.

They met at Bear Valley Creek in late July, 1935. They planned to use their remaining two boats, Alt's *Lota Ve* and Dr. Frazier's boat, for this trip renamed the *Helldiver*. But the Middle Fork in this stretch is a small, tight river, and to make matters worse, this was a low-water year. They started on July 17, and made only seven miles the first day. Alt noted that the river "was one continuous rapid and too shallow and rocky to get boats through without pushing and leading." Cap said it "was like running a wheel-barrow down a stairway to put a boat through this canyon."[14]

After only a few days, the bottoms of the boats were worn out. Twice Bus and Cap split small pine trees to make patches for the bottoms, but it really didn't do any good. At Sulphur Falls (since renamed Dagger Falls), they were faced with a real dilemma. At that stage of water, the rapid was impassable and they couldn't line due to ledges on both sides of the river. Just then three cowboys, who were moving a herd of cattle around the mountain, rode up, so the boaters asked them to help get their boats around the rapid. It was a good idea, and with the help of the horses, they had the boats around the falls in a few hours; lining would have taken them days otherwise.[15] It was probably the first time a rapid was negotiated by horsepower.

But at that point, just four days into the trip, they were forced to concede that they just weren't going to make it. It had taken them that long to go just ten miles; at that rate, they would be until the winter getting all the way through. After talking it over, they decided to cache the boats at Dagger Falls for the winter and come back earlier the next summer for another try. After hiking out to a ranger station, they hired a packer to come and get their supplies and what gear they didn't leave with the boats. They left the river vowing to make it all the way in 1936.

When they met again the next year on July 7th at Bear Valley, they were better prepared for what they knew would still be an arduous voyage. Over the winter, Bus and Cap had made two new boats, hopefully more suited to the tight channel of the Middle Fork. They were smaller, only fourteen feet long, and were open, not decked, to reduce weight. Cap later remembered that they "were light as a cork," and were very maneuverable. The bottoms were made of ¾ inch plywood for strength, and the sides were waterproof masonite.

They rode from Bingham, Utah, where everyone met, to Stanley, Idaho, in a school bus. On the way, Frank asked Bus if he had any money to buy whiskey. "Go to Doc [Frazier], Bus replied, 'he's your pal. Get the money off him." Dr. Frazier was asleep, so Frank rolled him over and too $20 out of his wallet. When Frazier sleepily asked him what it was for, Frank said it was to buy whiskey. "Aw, the devil with you—that stuff's no good," he said to Frank. At the next stop, Frank bought four gallons of whiskey. Although they did have a drink now and then, he actually had something else in mind. Central Idaho was, and is, a remote area, and whiskey would in both in demand and in short supply, so Frank used the whiskey to trade for flour and other supplies with the homesteaders along the river. As he later commented, "That whiskey was the finest thing we had on the trip. When we ran out of stuff we needed, we could get it. We had plenty of likker [sic] left when we got to Riggins."[16]

They trailered the boats into Bear Valley, arriving about ten days earlier than they had the year before. Luckily, the snowpack in the Sawtooth Mountains, the source of the Middle Fork, was heavier, and the low water that had defeated them the year before would not be a factor on this trip. With them this time were two new men, Dr. Wallace Calder, a dentist from Vernal, and Austin Lightfoot, the hunting guide. Loading the boats with just enough supplies to get them to Dagger Falls, Bus rowed one of the new boats with Dr. Calder, while Frank Swain rowed the other, accompanied by Lightfoot; the rest of the party traveled to Dagger Falls by horseback. In just a day and a half, they made it all the way to Dagger Falls with no problems. The new boats performed beautifully.

They camped there to await the rest of the party. Lightfoot was ill, and

rested under a tarp, while Frank cooked dinner and Bus went fishing. When Bus came back, he brought not only fish, but another prospective crew member, as Frank later recalled:

> Pretty soon here he comes back with the fellow with long, black whiskers, and [Bus] says "Look, Frank, look what I found up the river. He says his name's John Marshall. … this crazy son of a bitch was gonna jump off that bridge up there and commit suicide, and I talked him out of it."[17]

John Marshall, known as "Blackie," was a native of Iowa who had lived in Idaho since he was a child. That year, Blackie's fiancée, a pretty red-haired schoolteacher from Murtaugh, Idaho, had decided that she didn't love him, and had run off and married another man. Seeking a way to forget his troubles, he decided to float the Middle Fork in a homemade boat. Accompanied by a friend of his parents, O.W. Hestwick, he had started just a few days before Bus and the others, but had wrecked the canoe in the first rapid. When Blackie told Bus this sad story, Bus invited him for supper. Over the fire, Lightfoot revealed that he wasn't up to the trip, so Frank asked Blackie if he would like to come along, adding "We'll kill you and it won't cost you a cent." Blackie agreed enthusiastically.

The rest of the party arrived the next day, and Lightfoot and Hestwick left with the packer. While the others portaged the boats and supplies around Dagger Falls—the only portage of the trip—Bus and Cap worked over the *Lota Ve* and the *Helldiver* to get them into shape for the rest of the trip. Dr. Frazier had brought along conveyor belting from the copper mine in Bingham, to help protect the boat's tender bottoms from the worst of the rocks. This thick rubber belting was about three feet wide and strong enough to withstand being covered with ore. Bus and Cap nailed it to the bottoms of the boats, repaired and tarred any other cracks and leaks, and they were ready to go.

The trip went smoothly for the first few miles. The new boats were working out fine, the water level was better than the year before, and the scenery was on a grand scale. The clear water, abundant game and fish, and cool temperatures were a far cry from the hot desolate Grand Canyon. The Middle Fork was much more like Red Canyon and Lodore, and everyone felt more at home. In a letter sent out at the midpoint of their trip, Dr. Frazier waxed enthusiastic:

> Boys have we got this river under our belts! The two old boats are in good shape and with new bottoms we should have very little trouble making it from here on out. The river is a little lower than we had planned but with Frank Swain and Bus Hatch as lead-off men, the rest of us should be able to follow. This Vernal crowd is some water outfit and are by far the best fast-water boatmen in the world.[18]

Dr. Frazier's enthusiasm notwithstanding, the Middle Fork is a swift and rocky stretch of river, and they did have their share of spills. Alt tipped Dr. Calder out on July 10th; the next day it was Frazier and Bill Fahrni's turn. The 12th it was Alt's turn again—he pinned his boat against a rock and it took two hours to get it off. Everybody was skinned and bruised up from freeing and righting their boats when they had a mishap. In one such spill, their flour got soaked, as Dr. Frazier had packed it in paper bags. At one of the many ranches along the way, they were able to trade whiskey—which they had in abundance, thanks to Frank Swain—for flour. Frank was, as usual, the head cook, and everyone commented on his sour dough biscuits. Bus, also as usual, was off with his fishing pole as soon as they stopped, and kept the camp supplied with trout and salmon the whole trip. They ate better on this trip than they ever had on the river. At many places along there river there were hot springs, and they enjoyed hot baths frequently, a real luxury for river travel.

On the 15th, they came to the head of the Impassable Canyon, the last forty miles before the Middle Fork meets the Main Salmon. Here the river cuts through the Idaho Batholith, and the gorge is narrow, with steep granite walls. In places it is actually deeper than the Grand Canyon. Several ranchers along the way had warned them about this stretch of river, and they camped at the head, so they could have all day to get through it. About halfway down in the canyon, however, they spied a small cabin on the right bank. Stopping to investigate, they were surprised to see a note pinned on the cabin saying that nothing inside should be touched. Intrigued, they followed a trail behind the cabin, determined to see where it led to. A Mrs. Crandall, who lived in a ranch at the head of the canyon, had told them that a hermit lived down in Impassable Canyon. Perhaps the trail might lead to his cabin.

The trail went straight up the side of the canyon, snaking along narrow ledges and following shaky log ladders. After climbing over 2,000 feet out of the canyon they finally came out into a beautiful hanging valley. A little farther on was a dugout cabin, surrounded by a beautiful fenced garden. They knocked on the door, noticing that a note above the door said that "some of everything in this garden is poison." When no one answered, they sat down in the shade to wait. After a while a voice startled them from over their heads: "What do you want down there?" Looking up, there was a man sitting on a platform in the pine tree right behind them. The hermit scampered down the tree and eyed them suspiciously. A .45 revolver dangled from a string tied to his bib overalls. Frank Swain finally broke the silence and the tension, saying "Dad, you sure have a beautiful place here." All relaxed then, and the hermit of Impassable Canyon opened up a bit. His name was Earl Parrott, he told them, and he had been there since about 1917. He only went to the outside world once a year, for salt and cartridges for his .45. The gun, he told them, was not for bears or robbers, but in case he broke his leg in the woods somewhere. When he found out they were going down the river, he offered them strawberries and vegetables from his garden, which they were only too glad to accept. He accompanied them back to their boats, arriving back on the bottom of the canyon twenty minutes before the rest caught up with him. There they all sat down to a meal of his fruit and vegetables, along with trout that Bus had caught. As they got ready to leave, he startled them by asking "Who's going to run against Roosevelt this fall?" When they told him the Republican nominee was Alf Landon, Parrott said he would hike out of the canyon just to vote for him, since the CCC had built a trail 30 miles downriver from his home, and he blamed President Roosevelt for the intrusion on his privacy.[19]

After leaving the hermit, they floated on down to the mouth of the Middle

Fork, and camped for the first time on the Main Salmon. They were relieved and happy; this stretch of the river had been known to boaters since the 1870s at least. It was still rocky and had rapids, but from here on they expected relatively clear sailing. Dr. Frazier wrote in one of his rambling letters that "the expedition will turn into a vacation party at the confluence." But the trip wasn't over with yet, and this stretch of river was not known as the River of No Return for no reason.

Drifting along a day or so later, they surprised a large mother bear and her cub on the right bank. Immediately all hands decided to see if they could capture the cub, and began maneuvering to separate the mother from her cub. They were intent on this project, with Frank and Dr. Frazier in the lead, and Cap and Bill Fahrni hot on their tail, when they realized that they were on the brink of Big Mallard rapid, one of the worst on the Main Salmon. Desperately they tried to row back into the safe channel, but it was too late. First Frank and the doctor capsized over a big rock, and then Cap and Bill Fahrni. Fahrni swam after his hat—he was "bald as an egg," and needed the hat—not noticing that Cap hadn't come up. He was trapped under the boat; somehow a five gallon can had gotten over his head and shoulders. Worse, when the boat flipped it had come down on his right leg.

Bus saw what was happening, and "casting all precautions to the winds, he

dashed to our rescue, only to capsize himself on the first large boulder." Only Alt and Dr. Calder, bringing up the rear, were able to run the rapid safely down the right side. Cap, meanwhile, freed himself from under the boat, gotten it loose and towed it to shore. Only when he tried to stand up did he collapse in pain. Dr. Frazier examined it, and confirmed that the leg was fractured. Unfortunately for Cap, the plaster that Frazier had brought along for such emergencies had gotten wet and set up. All he could do was splint the leg and take over as boatman. Cap endured three days of pain before they reached their take-out at Riggins, Idaho.[20]

Despite this ending to their voyage, all agreed it had been a great success. Dr. Frazier was particularly enthusiastic and immediately made plans to repeat the trip the next year. The *Lota Ve* and the *Helldiver* were all but worn out, so during the winter Bus and Cap made the doctor two more boats like the smaller ones that had worked so well. As it turned out the next summer, however, both Bus and Cap were working on a construction job at Bonanza, southeast of Vernal, and couldn't get away for the 1937 trip. Frank Swain was the only experienced boatman on the crew, which included Frazier, Bill Fahrni, Blackie Marshall, and Hack Miller, a writer for the *Deseret News*, a Salt Lake City newspaper.

When they arrived at Bear Valley to start their trip, the water was much higher than they had seen it the previous two years. They launched their boats, but after a couple of days, Frank decided that it was too dangerous to go on,

and the others reluctantly agreed. Blackie Marshall left to find a packer to haul
their boats and supplies back out to town. That night, as they waited for him
to return, Dr. Frazier nursed his whiskey, moody and depressed. Finally he got
up, took a hatchet, and chopped holes in the boats. When the story by Hack
Miller appeared in the *Deseret News*, he blamed the failure of the trip on the
boats, which he said were poorly built and inadequate. No mention was made
of Dr. Frazier's fit of pique.[21]

Bus never forgave Frazier for this unwarranted criticism of his workmanship.
The boats were obviously every bit as good as they used in 1936—Bus never
did a job without doing it to the best of his ability. But Bus and Frazier had
never gotten along that well anyway—Frazier's bombastic style and hunger
for publicity had rubbed Bus the wrong way from the beginning—and this
incident was the last straw. The two never again had much to do with each
other. Frank was tarred with the same brush as Frazier in Bus's eyes for a
while, but as always, family ties were stronger than ruffled feelings, and Bus
and Frank were soon friends again. Frazier made a few more river trips, on the
Yampa, Glen Canyon, and the Middle Fork, and in 1940 went to the Antarctica
as Admiral Byrd's surgeon. Bus went back to Vernal, to his beloved mountains
and river bottoms, and to his family.

Even though he and Frazier parted ways after the Middle Fork trip, their
relationship had one good and long-lasting result. The idea of taking paying
passengers down the river had formed in Bus's active mind, and the more he

thought about it the more he liked it. All of the trips they had been on up until Frazier joined them had been strictly on a cost-sharing basis. There was no thought of making a profit; they were just a bunch of buddies going down the river to have a good time. When Frazier came along, he could afford to finance the entire trip, and they got paid to have a good time. Why not, Bus thought, recruit passengers and charge them a fare, and turn a pleasant pastime into a pleasant little business? Bus's main income was still from his contracting business, and would be for many years to come, but the extra money that came in from guiding river parties would come in handy. There have been very few river runners to this day who didn't have this same thought at one time or another; but in this, as in so many things, Bus was a man who could turn his dreams into realities.

By the end of the 1930s, Bus was generally recognized as one of the premier river runners on the Green. There were others who vied for the title, or sought the publicity such recognition would bring, but Bus did neither. He cared little for honors, and less for recognition. It wasn't in his makeup. When other river parties passed through Vernal, they always stopped at the Hatch house to seek his advice about the river. And they were always welcome. Many times Bus and his family would give up their beds so the visitors could be comfortable, and all visitors enjoyed the late nights around the Hatch table, passing a bottle and swapping river stories until all hours. Bus was always ready to run a shuttle, or haul a boat to the river with his truck, and to him it didn't matter who ran what river first, or who made the best run of a rapid. He liked running rivers, and he enjoyed the camaraderie that develops among those who run them. A man's actions always spoke louder than his words, and Bus Hatch had long since proved that he knew more about running the river than anyone else. Bus would one day start to take paying passengers down the river in earnest, and bring his whole family into the business, but that would have to wait a few more years. In the meantime, there were still houses to build, fish to catch, and rivers to run.

1 The "First Hundred" through the Grand Canyon, a benchmark for Colorado River historians and boatmen, was not reached until 1949.

2 Speculation about what happened to the three men ranges from their being killed by Shivwits Indians to their being murdered by the local Mormon militia. Aside from a single inscription on a remote mountain on the North Rim of the Grand Canyon, no trace of them was ever found.

3 "Four Vernal Men Navigate Yampa Gorge," *Vernal Express*, 7 June 1934. p. 1

4 "Boat Trip Down Gorge of Big Value," *Vernal Express*, 12 July 1934. p. 1

5 "Vernal Party Start Daring River Trip," *Vernal Express*, 19 July 1934. p. 1

6 Alton Hatch diary, July 19 – August 7, 1934. Hatch papers. Soap Creek was the last major rapid to be successfully run in the Grand Canyon, by Clyde Eddy in 1927.

7 Bus Hatch interview.

8 Mowrey interview.

9 Their macabre find created a minor historical tempest that lasts to this day: did the skeleton have a skull when they found it, or was it headless? Accounts differ; Dr. Frazier was later to claim that it had no skull, although the description of long black hair would seem to indicate it had. Both Dr. Frazier and Clyde Eddy later claimed that there was no skull with the skeleton, but in a letter from Don Hatch to Otis Marston, dated 5 April 1971, Don wrote: "Asked [Cap Mowrey] about the skeleton at Vasey's. Cap said he found the skeleton, called Dr. Frazier over to see it, eventually all saw it. He also pointed out these interesting things: The skeleton was complete with head. Both legs were broken just below the knees. A fire had been built in his stomach cavity out of 'Spanish bayonet' brush. The skeleton had no odor. The skeleton had been there a long time. The skeleton had long black hair; Cap assumed it was an Indian. The crew took nothing from the skeleton. Cap contends that Dr. Frazier made a trip via land into Vasey's the next year – using ropes, he, Frazier, took the head from the skeleton. (Frazier made the trip down into the canyon 'with another man.')"
   In his reply to Don, written 10 April 1971, Marston repeated Frazier and Eddy's claim of a headless skeleton but also writes: "Interviewing Frank Swain at Copperton [Utah] 7 May 1950 he stated that Joe Berger, Copperfield, has Skull from Vaseys. He thot [sic] Berger had gone to Vaseys with Frazier via House Rock valley.... In a letter to [Julius] Stone, 12 April 39, Frazier told Stone he was going down into Paradise Canyon [i.e., to Vasey's Paradise] on the 19th to be gone about 4 days." In the same letter, he writes that Charles Kelly, a Utah historian, had said in 1970, "that the skull of the skeleton was clearly shown in the movies that Frazier made. A later letter from

Kelly confirmed and said that Frazier brot [sic] the skull back." It makes sense to this historian that Frazier, a medical man, would have taken the skull, but no trace of it has ever turned up, unless it was the "fragmentary human skull" sent to archeologist Dr. Robert Euler by Frazier's family after Frazier's death in 1968. The skeleton was gone by the 1980s, according to *Over the Edge: Death in Grand Canyon*, by Michael Ghiglieri and Thomas M. Myers (Flagstaff, Arizona : Puma Press, 2001).

10 Alt Hatch diary.

11 Frederick S. Dellenbaugh, who had been on Powell's 1871 crew and was a great admirer of Major Powell.

12 The plaque at Separation Rapid had an interesting history. The original that Bus had made was covered up by the rising waters of Lake Mead. Frazier later motored up Lake Mead with another plaque, and affixed it to the rock walls. Later it too was almost covered up, so it was moved yet again, up the canyon wall to a spot where it was above the high water line, and there it remains to this day. Nor was this the only plaque they put up on this trip. While they were resting at the South Rim, a woman approached Dr. Frazier about placing a plaque near Horn Creek Rapid, where her husband, Fred Johnson, had drowned along with Park Ranger Glen Sturdevant in 1929. Bus made another plaque and they put it up as requested, but this plaque is now nowhere to be found.

13 Cap Mowrey later commented that he could never again eat pork and beans.

14 Alt Hatch diary, July 16-18, 1935; July 8-19, 1936

15 The story about the cowboys helping them line their boats is in the Alt Hatch diary for 1935, but Johnny Carrey and Cort Conley, in *The Middle Fork and the Sheepeater War* (Cambridge, Idaho : Backeddy Books, 1980) say that they cached their boats above the falls.

16 Interview with Frank Swain by Otis Marston, Copperton, Utah, 29 May 1948.

17 Undated interview notes with Frank Swain.

18 "Vernal Rivermen Make First Lap of Expedition," *Vernal Express*, 16 July 1936. p. 1

19 "Vernal Rivermen Successfully Navigate Idaho 'River of No Return'," *Vernal Express*, 6 August 1936.

20 IBID. Resourceful carpenters that they were, they built a box around Cap's leg and padded it with clothes.

21 *The Middle Fork and the Sheepeater War*, Johnny Carrey and Cort Conley. p. 15-16

Let's Take The Worst Places, Bus

EVEN THOUGH Bus spent a great deal of time organizing and participating in the big expeditions on the Colorado and Salmon Rivers, he still found time to pursue his favorite pastimes, fishing and hunting, and even to get in a shorter river trip or two. In October of 1934, Bus and Henry Millecam, a local dentist, led a large party of men from the Utah State Planning Commission and the Utah Museum of Natural History on a fishing and photography trip into Jones Hole. Bus was driving the lead car, a Dodge, and as usual was driving too fast for the rutted dirt road over Diamond Mountain. The low-slung car bottomed out in a rut, knocking the plug loose from the oil pan.

> There was a furious honking of the horn of the following car. Thinking they were unable to hold themselves on the hill, we speeded up, under the false impression their brakes were not holding; the din of horn and yelling told us something else was wrong. Bus got out, and there was our oil, dripping away from us, 30 miles from nowhere. Bus and [Grant] Cannon got under, and by some adroit calking made the old boat ready for the next rapids. Soon some sagebrush stumps yanked the calking out again. But Bus and Grant fixed it up again, and also a third time, so that we gave the title of "Our Little Fixers."[1]

The party finally got to the Ruple cabin at the head of Jones Hole Canyon, and hiked down into the Hole to camp. The truck bringing the bulk of their supplies had meanwhile burned out a bearing on the road, and they had only brought a little food with them. Then it started to rain, and continued to drizzle all night. Bus was at his best at times like this; he had a real talent for making circumstances that would normally ruin such a trip—car problems, no food, rain—seem like nothing. He caught a big mess of trout for supper and breakfast, and despite the bad weather and the mishaps on the road, all had a fine time.

Despite (or perhaps because of) the deepening Depression, Bus spent all his spare time fishing and hunting to add to the family larder. He still was able to get on the river for short trips, after the summer construction season was past, and as often as he could took one or more of his sons along. By this time he and Eva had four boys: Gus was born in 1924, Don in 1928, followed by

Frank in 1930 and Ted in 1933. As soon as they were old enough, Bus began to teach his sons the ways of the outdoors and the hows of the river. Sometimes it was just him and Eva; in October, 1935, the *Vernal Express* reported, Bus and Eva floated from Browns Park to Island Park during hunting season, "hunting their buck from a boat.[2]"

About this time Bus started taking the family down the Yampa River every year; this became a family tradition. They always stopped to visit at the ranch of Charlie Mantle in Hell's Canyon. Bus would bring in supplies and mail to the isolated ranch, and take out letters to be mailed. He even made a boat for Charlie Mantle, to use in herding his cattle and horses back and forth across the river.

Also in 1935, an accident occurred which almost cost Bus one of his brothers. Tom, Dr. Frazier, Bill Fahrni, and Dr. James Jensen, a dentist from Bingham, took Frazier's boat up to the Weber River, a mountain stream near Ogden, Utah, to get in some practice before the planned trip down the Middle Fork. "The boat had hardly started its trip when it struck a rock and overturned. Its occupants were hurled into the boiling torrent," an article about the tragedy related.[3] The others were thrown free, but Tom was swept into some rocks and pinned. He was able to save himself by holding his arms in such a way that it created an air pocket, but it was a very close thing. Bill Fahrni and Dr. Frazier made it to shore, and when it looked as though Dr. Jensen—the only one among them with no river running experience—was safe, they concentrated on saving Tom. His rescue took almost half an hour, but he was finally extricated with only minor injuries. But when they looked for Dr. Jensen, he was nowhere to be found. He was last seen floating downstream, acting "as though he was enjoying the experience. [He] floated on his back for a considerable distance, smiled at [a rescuer on shore], and apparently was disporting in the water." Just below that point, however, Dr. Jensen was swept under a rock and drowned. It was Tom's last river trip.

In 1936, after the successful trip down the Middle Fork, Bus and Frank Swain were contacted by three wealthy excursionists from southern California, who were looking for a river guide. Dr. Robert Langley was president of the Southern California Medical Association; Dr. H.V. Briesen was chief surgeon at a Los Angeles clinic, and Max Hebgen was a Hollywood broker. "Having heard broadcasted the beauties of the Green River gorges," the trio wanted someone to take them down the Green River, in what the *Vernal Express* mistakenly called "The first purely excursion trip to be made from Flaming Gorge down Green River to Jensen." Bus's fame as a riverman had begun to spread.

For the trip, which started on September 29, 1936 from Green River, Wyoming, Bus rowed one of the old open boats, and Frank rowed the *Lota Ve*. All of their provisions were stored in the compartments of the latter boat. The passengers brought along several expensive cameras and "1000 feet of film" to record the beauties of the canyon. Things went well until they reached Disaster Falls in the Canyon of Lodore. After Bus rowed the open boat through, Frank made his run. But he missed the proper chute. The *Lota Ve* crashed into a rock and capsized, finally becoming lodged against a mid-stream rock.

> The crew, working for 2½ hours in water and rain, could not recover the boat. To secure their food and other duffle stored within the compartments, it was necessary to use axes to break them open. The flour was made dough, and between all, there were but 20 matches left for the remaining four days of the trip. Staying there that night, drying out bedding and clothing around five fires, all their belongings were then packed aboard the open boat in which five must now ride, the trip was resumed.[4]

Bus must have felt real pangs of sorrow as he chopped holes in the *Lota Ve*, on which he had lavished such care, and which had carried him and his mates down so many miles of wild river. In a way, though, it was a fitting end to a boat that had seen five major trips on the Green and the Colorado, and logged probably 1300 river miles in its short life.[5]

From that point, the excursion turned into an ordeal. The old boat leaked water so badly that one of them had to bail almost constantly. It rode so low in the water that they had to portage three times, and were in constant danger from submerged rocks. Twice they hit with such force that Bus "was catapulted into the water headlong, to the amusement of the crew."[6] But again, despite the loss of the *Lota Ve*, and the loss of some of their film in the upset, the three California excursionists were loud in their praises of the canyon—and of Bus Hatch.

During 1937, Bus wasn't able to spend much time on the river, although Alt Hatch and Cap Mowrey ran the Yampa with Dr. Frazier, Hack Miller, historian Charles Kelly, and others. Bus was supposed to go on the trip, but was unable to make it at the last minute. He did get to make one run on the Yampa in the spring of that year. Esther Campbell was living at Teepee Springs, above the Yampa, with her husband Deward. They had gone down to the river to look for some stray cows, and she remembered seeing Bus, Eva, and Dr. Calder of Vernal, along with his wife Doris, come through Teepee Rapid, one of the

biggest on the river. Doris Calder was holding onto the boat with one hand, and her .22 rifle with the other, when she was thrown over the side. She finally had to let go of the rifle in order to climb back into the boat.[7]

But times were hard, and getting harder, and Bus had a growing family to feed. The Depression was still on, and construction was down. At times Bus and his family would live in the carpentry shop, or in a tent in Dry Fork Canyon, near Vernal, and rent out the family house to make ends meet.[8] During these lean years, Bus's hunting and fishing skills, developed so well during his own childhood, often meant the difference for his family between eating and going hungry. Still, like many families during the Great Depression, they never felt like they were poor. There was plenty of game, and the close family ties between the Hatches and the Swains meant that if one member of the family had a windfall, it was immediately shared with the others.

Even though the construction business was depressed, Bus's reputation as a contractor was such that whenever there was work in Vernal, Bus was given the job. In the '30s he built the Catholic church in Roosevelt, and when the Central School in Vernal was built as a relief project, Bus was chosen as head of the construction crew. But if nothing was going on in Vernal or the surrounding communities, Bus worked wherever there was a job to be had, as so many did in those troubled times. One job would be over in Artesia, Colorado, just over the state line; the next might be in Salt Lake City or Bingham, Utah, near the copper mine. Frank Swain, who had moved to Bingham in 1930, was sometimes able to get Bus some work at the copper mine or in nearby Lark, Utah. That year, for instance, Bus rebuilt Bill Fahrni's store in Lark, which had

been destroyed by a fire. He also built several houses and other buildings for the Utah Copper Company. It was good work, but Lark and the Salt Lake valley weren't home. Every chance he could get, Bus took his old Dodge touring car and headed back to Vernal.

In November 1938, river running was front page news in Vernal. Buzz Holmstrom and Amos Burg passed through on their Green-Colorado expedition, and stopped off to visit with Bus before continuing. Another expedition on the river at the same time was the DeColmont-DeSeyne kayak party. The Frenchmen stayed with Bus and Eva, who gave up their beds so that the foreigners could be comfortable.[9] They later sent Bus an autographed copy of the book Bernard DeColmont published about their exploits.[10] Still others were in the news; Dr. Frazier and Julius Stone were motoring up Glen Canyon, to place a plaque at the Crossing of the Fathers, Roy DeSpain of Springville, Utah, was leading a wildlife survey through Lodore, and just a few months earlier, Norman Nevills had completed a highly-publicized trip through the Grand Canyon.

Around that same time, Bus was asked to take an engineering party through Split Mountain to look at the possible sites for "power and irrigation," which meant one thing: dams. What Bus thought of the possibility of a dam on his beloved river at this time was not recorded, but he must have thought it an ominous development. They had a great deal of trouble just getting to the

river—they had to get out and repair the washed-out road to Rainbow Park no less than fifteen times, and the car "finally settled down into a mud hole" a short distance from where they planned to launch. Once on the river, it only took them a little over two hours to run the entire canyon, but after walking the three miles from the boat ramp to the dinosaur quarry, they missed the last car of the day, and had to keep walking to a ranch, finally getting back to Vernal at 7:15 that night.[11]

That short jaunt only whetted Bus's appetite, for the next year he was on the water as soon as the ice was out in the Yampa. Bus and Eva, accompanied by Roy DeSpain and Wes Eddington (who had been boatmen on the wildlife survey in Lodore the previous year) and their wives, left Lily Park, Colorado, in early June, 1939. They were using two boats built by DeSpain, also a carpenter, for the wildlife survey party. In describing the boats, Bus proved that he appreciated good work.

> The new boats designed by Roy DeSpain of Springville, were more responsible than any other one thing for making the run of the rapids this time the most successful one ever made by any party with whom I have gone.[12]

In an obviously expansive mood, Bus went on to praise Eva and the other women who had gone on the trip, declaring "The intrepid ladies made the descent of every rapid, and sometimes I thought the party would have been better off if the women hadn't been so brave."[13]

It was a great trip for all of them. The water was high enough to cover the rocks in the channel, and there were no upsets or even near-misses. They stopped to explore caves and photograph wildlife, such as deer, bear, geese and "other denizens of this unfrequented canyon." The last night's camp was at Jones Hole, and as usual, Bus supplied supper in the form of a fine bunch of trout. Roy DeSpain returned Bus's earlier compliments, declaring "Those trout, fryed [sic] by such an expert as Bus, certainly hit the right spot." To cap off a wonderful excursion, they stopped at the Ruple ranch and added Mrs. Lily Ruple Evans to the crew, and took the elderly woman for her first ride through Split Mountain Canyon.

Nineteen-forty was another banner year for river running on the upper Green. That year Norman Nevills took a party of tourists from Green River, Wyoming, all the way to Lake Mead. They stopped on the way to the launch and spent the night with Bus, so that Norm (who had never been on the upper Green) could borrow a set of oars, and not incidentally, consult with Bus about the canyons and rapids. Nevills stored his truck at Bus's house, and later, when the Nevills party came out at Split Mountain, Bus met them below the mouth of Split Mountain Canyon and took over the oars of Nevills' boat, the *WEN*, while Nevills drove Bus's car into town. Later, Bus loaned Nevills an outboard motor to get him through the flat water of the Uinta Basin. Also on the river at the same time that year were Don Harris, who had once rowed for Nevills, and Bert Loper, the Grand Old Man of the Colorado. Loper had been around the Colorado River since before the turn of the century, and had been the head boatmen on the 1922 USGS survey of the upper Green. They were on a trip down from the source of the Green River, and also stopped in Vernal to say hello to Bus—the river running community was a small one in those days.

Buzz Holmstrom, one of the best of the early river runners, was at the time working for a reclamation crew in Echo Park. In June of 1940, Bus, Roy DeSpain, Wes Eddington, and an engineer from Salt Lake City, Leland Kimball, drove down into Echo Park with a boat on a trailer. Finding Buzz there, they promptly invited him and the Reclamation crew boss Red Kreager, himself an experienced boatman, to go with them to Jensen. The river was running full, from spring run-off. With high water, and two such fearless types as Hatch and Holmstrom rowing the boats, it was bound to be a wild trip, and it was. "Let's take the worst places, Bus," Holmstrom said; Bus was never one to turn down a challenge, and they pushed their boats and capabilities to the limits.

Buzz
Holmstrom
in 1938

In Split Mountain, they decided to try the hardest runs they could find, and record them on film. Bus set up a camera to film his attempt to run the right side of the second rapid, a tricky one at any water level. "Satisfying a desire to hit the roughest of the rapids, Bus headed his craft into the crest of the waves," an article about the trip reported.[14] Bus flipped, and was thrown into the swollen river. He scrambled onto the bottom of the boat, just in time for it to flip back right-side up and throw him back into the river. Red Kreager finally caught up with him a further three miles downstream and hauled him in. Anyone else might have been shaken by two flips and a four mile swim through in a cold, swollen river. But to Bus, a simple thing like a capsize was not taken as seriously as it is today. If you flipped your boat, you just caught up with it and turned it back over. Nothing to get excited about. River running was more fun, and more trouble, in those days. One thing did come out of the trip though; then and there they decided on a new name for the second rapid in Split Mountain Canyon: S.O.B.[15]

In the autumn of that same year, Bus built a new boat that he wanted to try out. So he called his boating companion from the previous year, Roy DeSpain, who was then teaching vocational arts in Springville, Utah, and said "Let's go down the river." DeSpain was only too happy to oblige, so he loaded up his boat, grabbed his friend Wes Eddington, and headed out to Vernal. The plan was

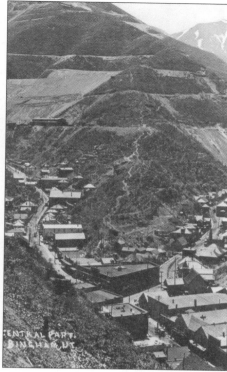

to float from Ouray, Utah through Desolation Canyon to Green River, Utah, hunting and fishing along the way. Wes Eddington had been with DeSpain in 1938, when they had met the DeColmont-DeSeyne party of kayakers in Red Canyon on the Green, and followed them all the way to Jensen. Eddington had been impressed by the Frenchmen's boats, sleek, maneuverable folding kayaks, and had ordered one from France. This was his first chance to try it out. Bus paddled it through some of the milder rapids, but didn't think much of the flimsy craft. His new boat performed well, however, as did DeSpain's. The only mishap occurred when they hung Roy's boat up on an exposed rock one evening just before they camped. But it was soon off, and the rest of the trip went smoothly. The deer and geese hunting was good; the fishing wasn't too good, but the whiskey they brought along more than made up for that and took the chill off the October nights as well. Above all, they were just glad to be back on the river.[16]

Just before World War II, Bus moved part of his family to Lark, Utah, to work for Utah Copper Co., overseeing construction and remodeling of mine

The Story of Bus Hatch

buildings.[17] Frank Swain, as always looking out for family, saw that there was construction to be done and recommended Bus. Bus and Eva and their two youngest sons, Frank and Ted, moved into a farmhouse a few miles below the mine in 1939. There was plenty of work at the mine as the copper company geared up to fill orders coming in from Europe, and for the first time in many years, the Hatch family knew prosperity. Many of the other members of the extended family were there also; Tom had married Bill Fahrni's daughter Maxine, and moved out earlier. Frank Swain had lived in Bingham since 1930, and Bus's other brothers—except Alt, by then assistant manager of the J.C. Penney store in Vernal—Cap Mowrey, and some of the Swains soon followed. Soon everyone worked at the mine on Bus's construction crew.

Working on a building near the mine one day, Bus's quick temper got the better of him. A steamfitter that Bus had hired, a big, burly man, borrowed $15 from Bus and promised to pay it back the next payday. Duff Swain, who was also living in Bingham at the time, told what happened next:

> Well, he never paid it. It went on for a couple of weeks, and finally Bus cornered him, and [the steamfitter] told him to go to hell, he wan't gonna pay him back. My brother Garn and Bus's brother Bay was standing there, it was on the steps of the *Lark Star*, that was run by old Bill Fahrni. And so Bus just reached up and slapped him the side of the head, and this big son of a bitch waded into Bus and they had a hell of a fight right there in the middle of the street. And he scoffed old Bus up a little. [The steamfitter] had a pair of

leather gloves, with a leather strip across the back and every time he hit Bus he's knocking the hide off him.

Later, when Duff and Cap Mowrey came home from Salt Lake, they found Bus quite a bit the worse for wear, with "little knots right along the front of his head, and skinned up here and there." Bay and Garn had just watched as the fight went on; when Duff asked them why they didn't intervene, Garn replied "Goddammit, Bus started the fight." That wasn't good enough for Duff; they could beat each other up, but when someone outside the family did so, it was a different matter. Bus's only comment, as he sat there nursing his cuts and bruises, was "I should've hit the son of a bitch in the mouth with a two by four. I slapped his face." He concluded, a bit ruefully, "We had quite a set-to." As Duff Swain later commented, Bus wasn't broke when he died, for the steamfitter still owed him $15.[18]

The quick reflexes that had saved him on the rapids of the Colorado and the Salmon stood Bus in good stead in other ways as well. One night, there was a boxing match in Salt Lake between a fighter from Vernal and a local champion. After they got off work, Bus, his brother Bay, with Garn and Duff Swain bought a gallon of port wine for $1.40 and headed into town to see the fight, at the old McCullough's arena downtown. Bus, who always liked fast cars, had bought a Lincoln touring car with a v-16 engine. It was over thirty miles from Lark to Salt Lake, and they were late for the start of the bout, so Bus floored the big Lincoln. Duff, who was in the front seat with Bus, remembered what happened next:

[W]hen Bus done anything, it was all out. He got in that son of a bitch and he opened her wide up and we got on that Redwood Road. And we went over to North Temple, and then headed east. And of course there's a railroad track there. Now he's doing about 80, coming down that North Temple street, and we's looking at the watch, and we had about like seven minutes to get to McCullough arena in time for this fight, see, and we was four miles out of town. All at once we heard a train whistle, just squealing. We looked up, and right there is this great big steam locomotive coming, with the smoke just laying right down over the cab, it was coming like a bat out of hell. Bus just took one look at that train; we're doing 80 miles an hour, there's no way on God's earth we're gonna stop, [so] he just stuck his foot in the carburetor. I'm not kidding you, we outrun that train so close, we had the [car] full of steam when we come out the other side.[19]

On top of their near miss, the Vernal champion lost the fight, and they drank up their jug during the match. They stopped at a beer joint on Redwood Road and North Temple on the way home, and consoled themselves arm-wrestling a couple of college wrestlers from the University of Utah for beer for the crowd. Bus, Duff, and Garn, their muscles hardened by years of construction work, won several rounds handily. The night hadn't been a total loss after all.

As America geared up for World War II, the Salt Lake valley was chosen as a center for training and supply bases because of its rail network, central location, and immunity from attack. A friend of Bus named Jim Orr was chosen to be the chief engineer of Camp Kearns, a sprawling overseas replacement depot west of Salt Lake City. More than 40,000 men were quartered there, and that meant a lot of construction and maintenance of buildings.[20] Jim and Bus had become close friends and drinking buddies when Orr was head of the CCC in Vernal before the war, and now he hired Bus as foreman of the construction and maintenance crews. Work at Camp Kearns was steady and paid well, and Bus stayed there throughout the war years.[21] As always, family was the most important thing, and he soon found jobs for whoever wanted to hire on. Garn and Duff Swain, Bay Hatch and Roy DeSpain worked for Bus at various times. Besides them, he supervised a crew a crew of forty men, and put up hundreds of barracks, supply warehouses, and other buildings.

He never forgot the call of the remote mountains or the river canyons, though. As often as he could get enough time off, and get enough gas ration coupons on the black market, he and Jim Orr would head east, to Vernal to hunt and fish, and occasionally run a river. Esther Campbell, who was teaching the Mantle children at their remote ranch along the Yampa in the spring of 1943, recalled that one morning she saw what appeared to be a log floating down the half-frozen river. As it came closer, she realized it was a wooden boat, and there were two men in it. Calling the children to help her—Charlie Mantle and the ranch hands were away at the time—Esther got the boat ashore and managed to get the two half-dead men inside the warm ranch house. They peeled their frozen clothes off, and warmed the bedraggled pair by the cook stove. As soon as Bus and Jim recovered enough to talk, they told Esther that they had gotten too far down the river to turn back when they had encountered an ice jam. In getting their boat around the jam, they had gotten soaked to the skin. The fact that all they had for food was whiskey and eggs didn't help their situation. Esther filled them full of hot coffee and food, and sent them on their way, shaking her head at such foolishness. Bus and Jim finished the trip without further trouble.[22]

The next year, Bus and Jim were back on the Yampa once again, this time to try the short but treacherous Cross Mountain Gorge, located in Colorado, above the main canyon. Cap Mowrey dropped them at the Grounds ranch above the gorge with one of Bus's boats, where they asked a Mr. Grounds for directions to the canyon. "Mr. Grounds gave them the necessary instructions but warned them that the canyon had never been run, and probably couldn't be run." Bus was skeptical, given his experience on whitewater, so they headed on down to the head of the canyon, and put their boat into the river early the next morning. As soon as they got in the canyon, Bus realized that the rancher was right: the canyon was impassable. The flood-swollen river shot over high ledges, gathered itself in swirling eddies, and plunged over another ledge. Bus told Jim that they had a 50/50 chance of making it through the first rapid, so while Jim made his way to the foot of the fall to help him land, Bus ran the boat through. He made it that time, but on the next 50/50 chance, the odds caught up with them. Bus was able to "shoot the specially built boat on top of a big boulder where it hung fast with the bottom and sides caved in." With the boat and most of their gear lost, Bus and Jim "then gave their entire attention to the matter of getting out with their lives." They spent the rest of the day trying to find a way out of the canyon, but the cliffs where they were stranded were unclimbable.[23] Jim looked at Bus, as they sat on the river bank, exhausted from yet another futile try to get out and said: "By God, Hatch, you don't have anything to kick about if we don't get out. You've led a well rounded out life." "You don't hear me kicking, do you?" was Bus's reply.

Cap Mowrey, meanwhile, had been waiting at the mouth of the canyon to pick them up. When he saw pieces of the wrecked boat come floating out, he feared the worst, and set off to put together a rescue party, which arrived about the time they finally got out of the canyon. After several more attempts, Bus and Jim were able to work their way around the cliffs in chin-deep water. Once past that obstacle, they found a precarious deer track that led to a way out of the steep canyon, and hiked six miles across the sagebrush to the ranch they had started from the day before.[24] The rancher looked at them long and hard when they came stumbling up, asking to borrow horses for the ride back to Vernal. Sure, he told them, he just happened to have a couple of thick-headed old nags—named Jim and Bus.[25]

The war years were not all death-defying high adventure for Bus, though; there were other, more conventional river trips. In May, 1942, a group of National Park Service archeologists and naturalists asked Norman Nevills to take them down the Yampa to search for ancient Indian sites. He referred them to Bus, who agreed to run the trip. This time Bus was careful, and the trip went smoothly. The scientists, who included luminaries from the Smithsonian Institution and the U.S. National Museum, besides the National Park Service, were loud in their praises of Bus:

> Piloted safely and expertly on the dangerous trip by Bus Hatch, noted river explorer of Vernal, in charge of the two boats, the scientific crew heaped praises upon him for his knowledge of river exploration. Assisting Mr. Hatch in the second boat was Tony [Roy] DeSpain of Springville, who has been with Mr. Hatch on other river trips. Water was very high and in places dangerous to run the rapids, Mr. Hatch stated.[26]

Sites investigated by the party included the Mantle Cave, near the ranch, which yielded some of the most important artifacts ever found along the Yampa.

But it was a party that Bus took down the river 1948 that had the most portent for his future, and the future of his beloved river. This group was from the Bureau of Reclamation, who wanted to examine potential dam sites along the river.[27] Several locations interested them, in Red Canyon on the upper Green, and in Split Mountain Canyon, but there was another potential site, just inside Whirlpool Canyon, downstream a mile or two from the confluence of the Green and the Yampa, that the engineers thought was the best of the lot. Here, it had already been decided, a dam would be built, that would realize the potential of the entire Uinta Basin. Bus's thoughts on this prospect are unrecorded, but the decision to place a dam there, in the heart of Dinosaur National Monument, would soon affect his life in ways he never would have dreamed.

endnotes

1 "Museum Men Taken Through Jones Hole," *Vernal Express*, 16 July 1934. p. 1

2　Local news section, *Vernal Express*, 24 October 1935.

3 "Vernal Boatman Nearly Drowned in Weber River," *Vernal Express*, 20 October 1935. p. 1.

4 "California Excursionists Praise Grandeur of the Green River Canyons, *Vernal Express,*
1 October 1936. p. 1

5 Shortly before he died in 1994, Don Hatch retrieved the stern compartment of the
Lota Ve; it is still in the possession of the family. Frank Swain "never ran Disaster
without Disaster," according to Bus, and did not successfully run it until 1958, when
he got through the rapid in a 10-man inflatable raft. Bus Hatch interview with Otis
Marston, 29 September 1958.

6 Things were not at all amusing between the two cousins, however, probably as a
result of the tensions between Bus and Dr. Frazier, with whom Frank Swain was still
friends. According to undated notes of an interview by Otis Marston with Frank
Swain, at one point Bus and Frank almost came to blows: "We were both mad but
we didn't have time to fight in the boat. He made a couple of passes and I grabbed
him by the hair and he couldn't reach me. Here comes the [others in the river party.
They said:] 'Okay, let it go.' Nothing had happened. Briesen saw Swain let go Bus's
hair. 'You think a lot of Hatch, don't you?' 'Yes, so much, I can't keep my hands off
him.'"

7 Esther Campbell interview, 11 March 1988

8 Frank Hatch interview, 4 April 1988.

9 Ted Hatch, only five years old at the time, nevertheless remembered sneaking out
of his bed late at night to listen to the strange talk, and admire the pretty French
woman, Genevieve DeColmont. Antoine DeSeyne, for his part, wrote in his journal
about how kind the Hatch family was to them, and about how Ted drenched everything he ate in ketchup.

10 The French Kayakers were front page news not only in Vernal, but up and down the
Green and Colorado Rivers. Bernard later sent out many copies of his book of pho-
tographs, titled "Les Voyagers Sans Trace"—Travelers Without Tracks,—to people
they had met along the river. For more about their journey see the *Utah Historical
Quarterly,* Summer 1987: "Les Voyagers Sans Trace: The DeColmont-DeSeyne Kayak
Party of 1938," by Roy Webb.

11 "Engineers Make Boat Trip Thru Split Mt." *Vernal Express,* 20 October 1938.

12 "River Expedition Reaches Jensen Sunday Evening," *Vernal Express,* 22 June 1939.
They also left their names and the date in Signature Cave on the Yampa, which is
across the river from the Harding Hole campground. The other two women were
Madeline DeSpain and Maria Eddington.

13 The same article describes Eva as a "veteran river runner," and she was not one
to back down from a challenge. That fall she was noted in the *Vernal Express* for
shooting a four-point buck. In November, she took the train all the way to Detroit,
Michigan, and drove back alone in a new car.

14 "Boat Overturns While Running River Rapids," *Vernal Express*, 13 June 1940.

15 *The Doing of the Thing: the Brief, Brilliant Whitewater Career of Buzz Holmstrom.* Vince Welch, Cort Conley, Brad Dimock. (Flagstaff, Arizona : Fretwater Press, 1998). p. 227. Also, Don Hatch letter to Otis Marston, 21 December 1961. Bus and his pards named all the rapids in Split Mountain Canyon. Moonshine, after Moonshine Draw, where they operated a still; S.O.B., as described; Schoolboy, because even though it looked difficult it was so easy a schoolboy could run it. Inglesby was named after Dr. Arthur Inglesby, the company dentist for the Utah Copper Company, who floated through Split Mountain Canyon in a wooden boat some time in the 1930s.

16 Roy DeSpain interview, 20 April 1985.

17 Duff Swain interview.

18 IBID.

19 IBID.

20 Thomas G. Alexander, "Brief Histories of three Federal Installations in Utah: Kearns Army Air Base, Hurricane Mesa, and Green River Test Complex," *Utah Historical Quarterly* 34 (1966):2.

21 The exception was his oldest son, Gus, who joined the Marines and was sent to the Pacific.

22 Esther Campbell interview, 11 March 1988

23 "Boatmen Risked Lives in Turbulent Cross Mountain Canyon," *Steamboat* [Colorado] *Pilot*, 6 July 1944. The next year, Bus found half the boat lodged on a sandbar just above Echo Park.

24 Bus Hatch interview, 1962

25 Don Hatch interview, 15 January 1988. See also "Boating on the Upper Colorado," C. Gregory Crampton Papers, Acc 727. University of Utah Library Special Collections. It is little wonder, from the stories of Bus and Jim, that some of the Hatch family felt that Jim was a bad influence on Bus. A group of hikers from Denver traversed Cross Mountain Gorge, on skates part of the way, over the ice in the winter of 1946, and claimed that they were the first to ever "conquer" the canyon, which might well have been true. ("Expedition Conquers 'Impassable' Canyon," *Rocky Mountain News*, February 20, 1946.) Cross Mountain Gorge was finally run in a kayak in the late 1950s by Walter Kirschbaum, one of the greats. A crew from Adventure Bound, Inc., ran it in a raft in 1974

26 "Park Service Completes Canyon Exploration Trip," *Vernal Express*. 11 June 1942. p. 1

27 "New Dam Sites Located On Green River," *Vernal Express*, 26 May 1948.

We'll Lick This Thing Yet: The Echo Park Dam

THE YEARS IMMEDIATELY FOLLOWING World War II were quiet ones for Bus. When the war ended, Camp Kearns was one of the first places to be closed down by the shrinking military. Bus was laid off, but it was just as well. He was tired of the Salt Lake valley, and longed for the mountains and canyons of his native eastern Utah. In late 1945, Bus packed up the family and moved back to Vernal.

A few years later, in the spring of 1948, they moved up to the Green Lakes Lodge, in the Uinta Mountains overlooking Red Canyon. There Bus and Eva managed the lodge and cafe, refurbishing some of the old buildings, stocking the fish ponds, and taking care of guests who came to stay at that beautiful spot. The whole family was there—Gus and his wife, Don, Ted, and Frank. It was a very popular attraction. There was fishing, archery, ping-pong, trail riding—they had a herd of twenty horses—and boats for rent, to use on the little lakes near the lodge. Ted remembered that on a holiday, such as the fourth of July, the lodge would be packed with guests.

One of Ted's jobs was to catch enough fish for the famous trout dinners offered by the restaurant. To do so, he used the old seine that Bus and his cousins had used years earlier at the mouth of Split Mountain Canyon on the Green River. They would throw the seine into the trout pond, pull it in, and gather up all the fish. One time Ted and Frank threw in the seine, but when they tried to pull it in, it was so full of fish that it was too heavy for the two of them. So Ted decided that horsepower was the solution, and hooked up old Buck, a working horse they used for rounding up the rental herd. Ted attached the ends of the seine to Buck's saddle horn, and started to back him up. But it was too much for the old net, and the weight of the trapped fish tore a huge hole in it. Unfortunately for Ted and Frank, Bus came home just at that moment. He had always warned them to be careful with the seine, and proceeded to blister their ears.

After the summer season was over, the owner offered to sell the lodge and property to Bus. The title to the property was unclear, however, and Bus was never cut out for such a life, anyway.[1] He moved back to Vernal and returned to contracting.

By this time Bus's son Don had moved to Salt Lake City, where he attended the University of Utah, earning a degree in education and eventually teaching sixth grade. He (and his brother Ted) became teachers so they would have their summers free and could help Bus take parties down the river. Bus's main income was still contracting; in 1948 he built the old Safeway store on Main Street and the Vernal Municipal swimming pool. River running was still just a pastime to him, although he did make a little money at it now and then. In May of 1948, for instance, he took a party of engineers from the Bureau of Reclamation from Echo Park down to Jensen to finalize their plans for the proposed dams on the Green. The engineers had their own boat, a barge that was specially built to haul supplies, crews, and core drilling rigs from their camp in Echo Park to the damsite. They had the boat, but they turned to Bus Hatch to run it for them.

There were also occasional trips for fishing parties, or to do work for the Park Service—at this time the Park Service had no boats or equipment of its own, and always turned to Bus whenever they needed some work done along the river. But river running as a business suffered from several drawbacks. For one thing, the wooden boats Bus was still using were completely unsuited for carrying passengers. Not that wooden boats weren't good for running rivers— Bus loved to work with wood, and produced some of the finest examples of wooden river craft ever to float the river. But they were relatively costly to build and maintain, and comparatively delicate. If you hit a rock hard enough, the boat would break. And, for the purpose that was growing in Bus's mind, they had one glaring fault: they could carry only a boatman and one or two passengers at most. Even then, passengers were forced to walk around most rapids, or if they insisted on running them, had to cling precariously to the deck. Not that many people would pay good money for that kind of ride.

Don Hatch remembered that his father had long before tried out a kind of hybrid boat, consisting of one of his later wooden boats with inflated bladders tied to the sides for stability. Along on this trip down the Yampa and Green were Don, his three brothers, Gus, Frank, and Ted, their uncle, and Bus. The idea was to beat the locals to the fishing at Jones Hole, "the easy way," as Don commented, but the water was extremely high. "[T]he river flooded its banks in Echo Park. Pool Creek looked like a lake." That volume of water made Whirlpool Canyon live up to its name, and the waves in the narrow canyon were towering; while his father ran a 5-horsepower outboard and oldest brother Gus ran the oars, Don and the younger brothers had to crouch in the bottom of the boat to keep the center of gravity low, and shift their weight to help stabilize the boat. They got to Jones Hole and fished for a couple of days, and then proceeded on down the river. In Split Mountain, the normal rapids were just about washed out by the huge volume of water, but as so often happens when the water level changes drastically, there were new ones. They finally ended up portaging the boat around one rapid below Schoolboy, where in a normal year there is hardly a riffle. But the hybrid boat performed beautifully, even with all that weight and in the high water conditions.[2]

Perhaps Don remembered that trip after World War II, when he started looking for a new way to run rivers, and urged Bus to look into the surplus sales that were going on at the time in Salt Lake City. The military was selling off vast stocks of surplus equipment, everything from trucks to guns to bridge pontoons, including 7-man and 10-man inflatable rafts, developed during the war as for use as life rafts, or for troops to cross rivers. Bus and Don realized that here was a replacement for the wooden riverboat. The inflatable rafts were cheap—only $25 each for a 10-man, less for a 7-man, complete with pumps, repair kits, life jackets, and paddles—and they were virtually maintenance-free. With an inflatable raft, you could carry twice as many passengers, and do it in comfort. If it hit a rock, it just bounced off. They required no varnishing or repairs beyond a patch or two now and then, and when the river season was over you could just roll them up and store them away. And they were so cheap that you could afford to have a fleet of them.

This was clearly an idea whose time had come, and several people started using them around the same time. John Cross, Al Quist, and Malcolm "Moki-Mac" Ellingson used 10-man rafts to take parties of Boy Scouts through Glen Canyon right after the war. Harry Aleson and Georgie White took rafts through the Grand Canyon, and Roy DeSpain, Bus's old river running buddy from the 1930s, started using them on the Green and Yampa just a few years later. Still, some river runners felt that they could never replace wooden boats, but Bus and Don were convinced otherwise, as an article by Don in *American Whitewater* magazine indicated:

> They handle extremely fast. They pivot, side slip, and perform many other antics not usually possible with other boats. An empty ten-man raft with a good set of oars can be made to almost leap out of the water with one good hard stroke. They turn and dodge like little water bugs. This is possible because they draw less than three inches of water—loaded! They bounce off rocks like a billiard ball striking a cushion. When they pound through big waves and holes, their low center of gravity helps tremendously to keep them upright.[3]

Here, at last, was a way to make a living running rivers. Bus and his son Don each bought a ten-man raft, and equipped them with a wooden rowing frame and a pair of sturdy ash oars. Their first trip with the new boats confirmed what Bus and Don believed: the rafts were great riverboats. They were easy to handle, rode the rapids well, and with their low center of gravity were much more stable than a wooden rowboat. The inflatable rafts were especially well suited to running in the later part of the season, slithering over exposed rocks in the channel that would wreck a wooden boat. Even mounted with a motor, the inflatable boats worked well, and best of all they could easily carry up to four passengers and a full load of gear.

The inflatable rafts had proven their worth as river craft—now all they needed were passengers. That was the other drawback to running a river business in eastern Utah. It was such a remote region that few people had ever heard of the Green and Yampa Rivers, let alone were interested in coming there for a vacation. Bus did no advertising, so all of his passengers came by word of mouth, as in the old days. Prices were certainly reasonable: for a six day trip, the fare was only $60.[4] Those who did run the river came away mightily impressed with the beauty and challenge of the canyons. But there simply weren't enough of them, so the river business grew haltingly.

There were others, however, who had their own ideas about the potential of the canyons of the Green River, and those ideas had little to do with boats and beauty and rapids. Soon after World War II, the Bureau of Reclamation announced plans for the Colorado River Storage Project, one of the most ambitious reclamation projects ever conceived. The project, as envisioned, would involve the construction of five major storage and hydroelectric units

Riverman

on the Colorado and its tributaries. The combined projects would store forty million acre-feet of water, and produce 1,650,000 kilowatts of electricity. Two of the dams were to be on the Green, within the boundaries of Dinosaur National Monument.[5] The smaller of the two was to be in Split Mountain Canyon, just above the big bend that marks the end of the canyon. It would flood the canyon, most of Rainbow and Island parks, and the lower end of Whirlpool Canyon, including Jones Hole.

The other dam proposed for Dinosaur was to be in the upper end of Whirlpool Canyon, where the canyons walls are deep and narrow. It was to be the biggest, most important dam in the whole project—the Bureau of Reclamation called it the "wheelhorse," or the "centerpiece" of the entire plan. The Echo Park Dam was planned as a 700-foot high concrete arch dam that would create a vast reservoir, flooding the Canyon of Lodore, Browns Park, and all of the spectacular lower Yampa Canyon. The city fathers of Vernal and the surrounding communities were delighted; here at last was a way to develop the Uinta Basin to what they saw as its full economic potential. They might even build a railroad![6]

Plans for the dam had been in the making since the 1920s. Bus, like all the residents of Vernal and the surrounding communities, had known about it for years, but even though he had taken several parties of engineers down the river for their damsite surveys, he was one of the few residents of Vernal to oppose

The Story of Bus Hatch

the project. The reservoirs would flood his beloved canyons, and end his river running business before it got fairly started. He didn't dare disapprove openly, though—his livelihood was building houses and other buildings in Vernal and the surrounding communities, and dam-fever was so high in the area that anyone who opposed the project was immediately branded a traitor to Vernal's future, a radical, even a communist. Bus kept his counsel, and remained silent.

Instead, Don became the voice of the family, openly announcing his opposition to the project. He was at once denounced by the citizens of Vernal, and told never to return. He received hate mail and threats, and was openly denounced on the city streets. While his mother fretted about her son's stance, Bus approved. In one letter to Don, written at the height of the controversy, Bus passed along some inside information about the dam and assured him "We'll lick this thing yet." Bus encouraged Don to continue speaking out against the dam and not to worry what the people in Vernal thought.

In the meantime, when anyone wanted to go down the river, Bus was there. In 1950, he took a group of men from the Echo Park Dam committee of the Vernal Chamber of Commerce down the river. They were all strong proponents of the dam, and the trip was "designed to investigate allegations that Echo and Split Mountain Dams would harm scenic attractions and wildlife." Naturally enough, they decided that the dam would do nothing of the sort, as an article in the fiercely pro-dam *Vernal Express* noted:

> [C]onstruction of the dams would add to scenic advantages of this area by making the Echo Park and [Split Mountain] Canyon areas more accessible, and that it would not harm game. According to Mr. [Harry] Ratliff they concluded that the submergence of the area is of little consequence when compared to the magnitude of such features above the water of the proposed reservoirs. Most wildlife finds its habitat up on mesas above the canyon walls rather than down in the gorge which would be filled with water backed up by the dam, the party observed.

In a parting shot that was a portent of the war of words soon to be declared, the article concluded:

> Members of the party expressed the opinion that they were more convinced than ever that propaganda being lavishly used by the National Park Service is false and is distorting facts.[7]

Echo Park Dam
will create a

PLAYGROUND
for MILLIONS

One of the arguments often used in favor of the Echo Park Dam was that the canyons were too dangerous and inaccessible to anyone but daredevils and adventurers. This idea that the Green River was too hazardous to float had long been a theme in Vernal, despite all of the parties that had run the river successfully for the past half century. The controversy over the dam only made it get worse. "This treacherous river-race is to be transformed into a lake with an average depth of 200 feet, making it perfectly safe for boats, large and small," one editorial in the *Vernal Express* noted. The writer then went on to incidentally give a plug to Bus for his river running business:

> Until the dam is constructed, it is hoped that river trips will be guided by competent river-men. Much credit is due to Bus Hatch and his staff of able boatmen, for the few accidents that have occurred with large groups being taken down the rivers. Light craft and unskilled guides may spell disaster when such groups approach they many places in the canyons where the river becomes a churned-up demon of destruction and terror.[8]

Weight was given to these kinds of arguments by a "fact-finding" trip consisting of a large group of engineers, geologists, and wildlife experts, taken through the Canyon of Lodore by Bus in May 1951. Bus rowed a 10-man raft, his son Frank a 7-man. Two other 7-man rafts were handled by Sammy Hatch, a cousin and Utah Highway Patrol trooper, and Bill Slaugh, a family friend. Also along on the trip were Harry Ratliff, a local supporter of the dam, Don Howard, a *Salt Lake Tribune* reporter, and Otto Roach, a photographer for the paper. The passenger list for this trip had the names of many other prominent men in Vernal, as well as members of the U.S. Fish and Wildlife Service, and the Colorado Fish and Game Commission. Billed as a "fact-finding expedition," the men were set to enjoy a few days of fun. However, the river had other plans, as they found out when they reached Disaster Falls. The water was extremely high for Lodore, almost 20,000 cfs. All the boats made it through the first small rapids in Lodore, but at Upper Disaster Falls, the troubles began. Bus was in the lead, and as soon as he came around the curve that marks the beginning of Disaster Falls, he realized that this would be no easy run. Don Hatch described what happened in a letter written a few years later:

> Perhaps you recall the almost disastrous trip made through Lodore in the late nineteen forties—or was it early fifties? On it were Harry Ratliff, chief organizer, Otto Roach I think, photographer, a *Salt Lake Tribune* man, some

Steam-
boat
Rock.
Conflu-
ence of
Green
and
Yampa
on right.
Dam
would
be
down-
stream
2 miles,
around
corner
on left

of the local Vernal men, etc. Well my brother, Frank Hatch, was running first and clowning it up plenty. Lodore had extreme high water, but the whole outfit hardly considered this. They ran the first riffles in Lodore easily (high water had smoothed some) but Upper and Lower Disaster was ahead, and still on that tricky little bend that catches the sleepy boatman out in the middle too far to land. Frank, too far ahead to hear any advice dad had to offer, hit Disaster flush on the hole. He had a 7-man boat with those extra bladder inflated side tubes I told you about earlier. Miraculously he rode it through without tipping. Most astounding was the fact that his motor (he was running a five h.p. old Johnson) was still sputtering and running. Dad's boat followed – a ten-man, and damned if it didn't ride it out too. But then came a boat handled by Bill Slaugh, local Vernal car salesman and garage man. He tipped over in his seven-man. Along came another boat handled by a Mr. Merrill, [of] Vernal. Merrill tipped over too—also in a seven-man. I think another boat followed [rowed by Sammy Hatch]. It tipped over.

Now you know the island (first one just below Upper Disaster). One boat ended up there. Frank's boat bounced on down through Lower disaster picking up baggage. Slaugh's boat ended upon the right side just before you get to the cliff section. (a very lucky thing for him too). All in all, everyone made it out O.K. Don't ask me how they did it in high water either, for the men weren't any spring chickens. Among the article salvaged was a pressure cooker full of stew. A fire and the stew gave them heart again. They finished out Lodore in a cautious manner, portaging a rapid above Triplet Falls which I call the Harp Rapids. And they portaged Hell's Half [Mile]. Dad ran all boats through bad rapids after the accident.

What really happen[ed] (my guess) is that the crew had too many bosses and too much B.S. as they drifted toward Upper disaster. Frank said 'So and so was supposed to watch the maps.' Some one else said 'blank, blank, was supposed to do this and do that.' Someone else was supposed to be a Bureau of Reclamation man—all knew before they got to Upper Disaster exactly where they were and exactly what they could or couldn't do. My, how the stories changed after the dunking. [9]

No wonder that the *Vernal Express* could editorialize about the Green as a "churned-up demon of destruction and terror."[10]

Despite this and other highly publicized mishaps, there were still people willing to float the Green and Yampa for the adventure. One of them was a young man from Colorado named Steve Bradley. Bradley was a native of Wisconsin who had gone to school at Dartmouth, where he had been on the ski team. After service in World War II, Bradley moved to Colorado for the skiing. There, in 1950, he became the manager of the Winter Park ski area. Soon after he moved to Colorado, Bradley became interested in kayaking. He and a friend, Dave Stacey, each bought a foldboat—fifteen-foot long collapsible kayaks—and took them to the nearby Cache La Poudre river, where they taught themselves how to handle a kayak. After a couple of years, they both became proficient, and started looking for a challenge greater than they Cache La Poudre's relatively mild rapids. Dave Stacey had heard of a man who took groups down the Green and Yampa Rivers, not far from where they lived, so they called Bus Hatch and asked if he would follow them down the river and carry their gear, while they paddled their foldboats. "Sure," Bus said, "if you want to risk your neck in one of those things I'll be happy to carry your duffle."

They met in Vernal in the early summer of 1951, and drove over the Uinta Mountains to a put-in on the Green at the Hideout Flat Forest Camp, near the head of Red Canyon. Dave Stacey and Steve Bradley each paddled their foldboats, while Bus carried their wives and all of the gear in a 10-man boat. There were only two rapids of any consequence on that stretch of river, Ashley Falls and Red Creek, but both were difficult enough. Both had tight, rocky channels, requiring precise maneuvering. And foldboats were quite delicate, ill-suited for rocky rivers. Just a month before the trip, in fact, Steve had wrapped his around a rock in the Cache La Poudre, and had had to get a whole new framework.

But both Steve and Dave made it through Ashley Falls and Red Creek without any mishaps. Bus was impressed. When they ran the latter rapid, Bus, who had gone ahead to make camp, met them at the shore with a bottle of whiskey. Offering them a drink, he declared that he was ready to christen them river rats. As they drifted along into Browns Park the next day, Bus regaled the passengers with tales of Butch Cassidy and the Wild Bunch, who hid out in the Park scarcely half a century before. He told them about Butch, and the dapper Sundance Kid; about his father's friend Speck Williams, the black man who took care of their hideouts when they were on a raid, and ill-tempered Charlie Crouse, who raised the fine horses they used.

In the lower end of Browns Park, a truck met them and ferried boats and passengers around to Lily Park, for a run down the Yampa. Bradley and the others were greatly impressed with this beautiful canyon, with its towering walls of smooth white sandstone. In the upper end of Whirlpool Canyon, about two miles below Echo Park, they noticed a series of ladders coming down the canyon wall all the way to river level. Steve asked Bus what they were for, and was shocked when Bus told him that this was the site of dam that would be built within the next few years, and would flood all of the canyons they had just come down. Bradley and the others had never even heard of this proposed dam, but they resolved then and there to fight it.

There had already been some scattered opposition to the Echo Park dam. At issue, its opponents felt, was much more than the lovely, but remote canyons of the Green and Yampa Rivers. Conservation groups opposing the project saw this as a precedent-setting action. If the Bureau of Reclamation could build a dam in a National Monument, they reasoned, was any area supposedly protected by the National Park system safe from development? The National Park Service itself was strongly opposed to the dams, but within the Department of the Interior, the Bureau of Reclamation's voice carried much more authority. From the first, proponents of the Echo Park Dam were confident of success. Never had there been any effective opposition to a western water project like the Echo Park Dam. Considering all the economic benefits the construction would bring, their reasoning ran, how could anyone be against it? As earnest and determined as the opponents to the dam were, they were far too outnumbered and disorganized to stop it. The Echo Park Dam looked like a sure thing.

Fortunately for the opponents of the dam, Steve Bradley had a well-placed ally. His father, Dr. Harold Bradley, had recently retired from the University of Michigan, where he was a professor of biochemistry, and moved to Berkeley, California. There he was elected President of the Sierra Club, the nation's oldest and most influential conservation group. Steve called his father and alerted him to what was taking place in Dinosaur. He suggested that they go down the river, take movies and photos, and see if they couldn't use them to stir up some opposition. Dr. Bradley agreed, so Bus took the entire family—Dr. and Mrs. Bradley, seven brothers and their wives—down the Green in 1952. All agreed that something must be done before this lovely area was lost forever.[11] Dr. Bradley, Steve, and his brothers returned to their various homes and began writing, lecturing, and showing their films. As the Bradley family spread the anti-dam word, others in the Sierra Club, especially the California branch, got interested in going down the river, and more importantly, in fighting the plans to build the Echo Park Dam in Dinosaur National Monument. The California chapter was probably the largest and most powerful of the 50-year old club's divisions. It was certainly the most politically active, as the Bureau of Reclamation and the supporters of the Echo Park Dam soon found to their dismay.

The leaders of the Sierra Club decided that in order to save a place, you needed to know something about it, so they decided to sponsor river trips down the Yampa and the Green rivers through Dinosaur. The Club had a long history of club outings, up until this time mostly hikes in the Sierra Nevada or other mountains. But this was something different. They had neither equipment nor experience for a trip down a wild river. At Dr. Bradley's suggestion the outing office contacted Bus and asked if he could take a group down the river. "How many?," Bus asked. About a hundred, was the reply. Bus gulped, but said "OK, we'll do it." The Sierra Club chartered a trip the next year, 1953.

Taking a groups of this size down the river was unlike anything Bus had ever done. Clearly two 10-man rafts would not be adequate for such a crowd, nor did Bus want to take a fleet of small rafts. Looking for an alternative, Bus bought several 27-foot bridge pontoons from Buck's Surplus in Salt Lake City. These huge inflatable ovals were designed by the Army to be hooked side by side across an unbridged river, or one where the bridges had been blown up. Then a roadway was laid over the top that could carry jeeps, trucks, even tanks. To use them as river boats, Bus built wooden frames that sat on top of the pontoons, and then equipped each with sets of oars at front and back. Thus equipped, the giant rafts could carry about a dozen passengers, and all their gear, down the river.

For crews to man his new boats, Bus turned to his family first. His sons Don, Ted, and Frank all helped out with the trips, rowing boats, running shuttles, packing food, and seeing to all the thousand and one details of running a successful river trip. When they were unable to help, he recruited local boys and college students looking for a different summer job. Bus's wife Eva was also involved, planning menus, then buying, sorting, and packing the huge amount of food necessary for such a large group.

The first Sierra Club trip in 1953 established a pattern that many similar club outings would follow for the next several years. The passengers met on the morning of the trip at the Hatch yard on 4th East Street in Vernal. One passenger described her fellow travelers as a "heterogenous and colorful collection of individuals," who "came in all ages, shapes and sizes, with a sprinkling of small fry for seasoning." On these early trips, they were mostly from California, although later that would change. The Sierra Club coordinator on many of the early Sierra Club trips was Glen "Brick" Johnson. After he introduced himself, he would in turn introduce the passengers to Bus, "that veteran of the boiling waters, that intrepid originator of river trips, that Dean of the boatmen."[12] Each passenger was given a black rubber waterproof bag to store their duffle, and then they loaded up into two old school busses that Bus had somehow procured, and were off for Browns Park for the Green, or Lily Park for the Yampa.

On the earliest trips, Bus and the boatmen rigged the boats while the passengers had lunch and stretched their legs after the long, jolting bus ride. Later, he sent the crew ahead to have the boats ready to go when the passengers arrived. Most of them were content to ride on one of the pontoons, but even then there were a few hardy souls who wanted to run the river on their own, and brought foldboats. After lunch, they were fitted with life jackets, and all the gear was stowed on board the pontoons. When all was completed, and they were assigned to a boat, Bus would say "Now we're safe, now we're on the river," and they would shove off.

In Lodore, Bus usually had the passengers walk around most of the rapids. At Disaster Falls, for example, the passengers would debark, and one of the boatmen would join Bus on the other set of oars in the front of the boat. They would then row the boat through, and re-load the passengers at the foot of the rapid. Occasionally, Bus would allow some of the more adventuresome ones to ride on the boat, but the big pontoons were so heavy already that it was all he could do just to maneuver it as it was, without the extra weight of passengers. One or more of the foldboats would inevitably crash in Triplet or Hell's Half

Mile. These early kayaks consisted of a rubberized canvas skin stretched over a wooden frame, and were much better suited for flatwater touring than for the tight, technical rapids and rock-choked channels of the Green. A sharp collision with a rock would usually reduce the boat to a bagful of sticks. Bus would pick up the chagrined paddlers, and they would continue. No one was ever seriously injured, although Don Hatch called the double foldboats "divorce boats," from the arguments that inevitably ensued between husband and wife teams. On the Yampa, the rapids were more straightforward, and such accidents were uncommon. Bus would usually let the passengers ride the pontoons all the way down.

Lunch usually consisted of cold meats and snacks and a pot of coffee. The Sierra Club would often bring their own commissary and cooks; if not, the boatmen had to prepare meals in addition to other duties. But there was still time for frequent stops, to explore places like Winnie's Grotto in Lodore, or Signature Cave at Harding Hole on the Yampa. Another regular stop on the Yampa was the Mantle ranch, to meet Charlie and Mrs. Mantle, and to hike up to the caves which contained artifacts left by the long-vanished Fremont Indians. Throughout the trip, those on Bus's boat were treated to a constant flow of lore about the ancient Indians, stories of the outlaws, and anecdotes about early river explorers. Camp would be in some beautiful spot like Rippling Brook or Harding Hole. After supper was over, the group would gather around a fire for singing, stories, or impromptu concerts.

Riverman

The last night's camp, always at Jones Hole, was the climax of the trip. They would get there early, so that everyone could hike, fish, or float through the little rapid on air mattresses, while Bus and the crew prepared a special treat, a lamb brought down from the end of the road for that last night's dinner. One passenger on a trip in 1957 described what many Sierra Club members had already experienced and would never forget:

> The very piece de resistance enroute was on the occasion of our last night in camp at Jones Hole when Bus Hatch treated us to a barbecued lamb; donated and prepared solely by him. The night before, a fire was kept burning constantly in a rock-lined pit so that the following morning there was a bed of live embers. With deft dispatch Bus made incisions in a good-sized lamb and inserted spices and seasoning, swathing it in a muslin wrapper. At mid-morning this "mummy," along with two roasts of beef, was placed on a wire cradle over the gleaming embers in the pit, a lid of tin sheeting clapped on and covered with earth; and then it was left to cook for seven hours of so (while we hiked, explored, fished or did as we pleased in those magnificent surroundings). Just as dusk was falling we gathered at the pit. There was a fanfare in the forest and out came a procession headed by Brick Johnson, blowing the bagpipes and sporting a beach-towel "kilt" with springs of box elder at elbow and knee, followed by Bus (elegant in a most colorful sport shirt, and brandishing a carving knife) and five of the most stalwart boatmen

shouldering spades and shovels. With due ceremony the pit was uncovered and opened, the savory contents exhumed and paraded off high on a plank to the Commissary area with proper pomp and reverence. How quickly and deliciously that carcass vanished![13]

Bus was in his element. Cooking elaborate meals, telling stories of the old days, skillfully navigating the rapids, he revealed a side of his character not before seen: the showman. For many passengers, Bus was the main attraction. Many people who would never dream of running a wild river would go with Bus, not only because they trusted his skill at the oars and his years of experience, but because they liked him.[14] Bus Hatch came to symbolize river running; you couldn't separate one from the other, because for most people, he fit the ideal image of a river runner as crusty, rough around the edges, his face lined by wind and weather. Here was the real key to Bus's success with the Sierra Club trips. His manner, his obvious skill, and his own love of the outdoors and the river shone through on every trip. Bus's grandson Tom, by then a junior boatman, remembered that his grandfather loved to tell stories, jokes, and tall tales to the passengers until all hours of the morning. "He couldn't sing, he couldn't dance, but he could sure cuss and tell stories."[15] Old and young alike could feel comfortable with Bus. After the first couple of trips, he didn't need to advertise; the testimony of hundreds of satisfied club members was enough to ensure him business for many years to come.

Meanwhile, the fight over the Echo Park Dam raged on into the 1950s. Scoffing at the "daredevil" arguments put out by dam supporters, the Sierra Club unleashed its own barrage of articles, maintaining that the opposite was true. Martin Litton, then a circulation man for the *Los Angeles Times*, went down the river with Bus in 1953, and wrote an article for the *Times* entitled "Children in Boats Run Utah Rapids: Californians Refute Claim That Wild Green River Is Dangerous." In the article, Litton described his young daughter and son swimming, fishing, camping, and having the time of their lives. In the lead paragraph he directly refuted the dam-builders claims, by quoting an editorial from the *Deseret News* that warned "[the Green River is] too inaccessible and dangerous for other than the most skilled boatmen." Litton wrote "When the above lines appeared in print my 4-year-old daughter and 7-year-old son were merrily riding rubber rafts through the ruggedest canyons the Green River has to offer—in the heartland of Dinosaur National Monument." Referring to the treacherous rapids, he wrote "They laughingly braved the roaring white water of the Green in Split Mountain and knocked into a cocked hat all the old bugaboos about insurmountable hazards." Driving his knife in a little deeper, Litton concluded that "Like other streams—like surf or stormdrain or bathtub, the Monument's rivers can be hazardous for the careless or inexpert."[16]

Angered, the *Deseret News*, which was rabidly pro-dam, fired back in another editorial titled "One more Dinosaur Myth Exposed." It admitted that children had gone down the river, but pointed out that "all these people were passengers, not river runners. A corpse could make the trip if Bus Hatch, ace riverman, wanted to take it through."[17] True enough, but the image of children cavorting on the Green River, that "churned-up demon of destruction and terror," was enough to shoot some substantial holes in the "daredevil" argument.

In the midst of this heat, Bus was benefited from both sides of the controversy, all the while remaining mum about his true feelings on the dam. In 1953 he took over 300 passengers down the Green and Yampa, including both pro- and anti-dam groups. Besides the Sierra Club, these included the Colorado Fish and Game Commission, the Vernal Chamber of Commerce, and a group from Yosemite National Park. The next year, he had almost 300 passengers in June alone, bringing that year's total to over 500. Nine more such trips were scheduled, the *Vernal Express* noted, and over one thousand people were expected to make the river run before the end of the season. These numbers continued to climb until the controversy finally died out.

Letters and comments from Sierra Club members who had gone down the river with Bus poured into Congressional offices, opposing the Echo Park Dam. But there were two other anti-dam screeds—one in print and the other on film—that capped the conservation efforts to defeat the Echo Park Dam. Neither could have come about without the cooperation of Bus Hatch. The first was an article about a March, 1953 river trip sponsored by the National Geographic Society, which was given full coverage in the March, 1954, issue of *National Geographic* magazine.[18] The Society wanted to investigate for themselves what the arguments were about, so they turned to the only man capable of taking them down the river, Bus Hatch. Bus, Don, and Boon MacKnight, a Vernal native, were the boatmen. Passengers included Jess Lombard, superintendent of Dinosaur National Monument, Park Service director Conrad Wirth, his assistant, and other Park Service officials. Even though the Park Service was a sister agency of the Bureau of Reclamation, they made no secret about their opposition to the dam.

For the first time, the general public was introduced to the wonders of the canyon of the Yampa, through the beautiful color photographs that *National*

Geographic is so justly famous for. At the same time the anti-dam message was subtly, if forcefully given. Thousands of people read that issue, and wondered if they could possibly try such an adventure. The answer, promoted heavily by the anti-dam groups, was of course they could. Thousands of people looked at those wonderful color photographs and saw "Hatch River Expeditions" emblazoned on the sides of the boats. No businessman could ask for better advertising, and free at that.

The other anti-dam message was much more overt and came in the form of two films by Charles Eggert, a resident of New York. A Navy photographer during World War II, he had a "spiritual experience" in the Grand Canyon of the Yellowstone River immediately after the war and decided that he had to use his skills for the conservation movement and the National Parks. He contacted various groups and was told to go west and get involved with the efforts to stop the Echo Park Dam. Eggert went along on some of the early Sierra Club trips with Bus Hatch, and made two films. For the National Park Service, he made *This is Dinosaur*. For the Sierra Club, he filmed and produced *Wilderness River Trail*. Both hammered home the anti-dam message in no uncertain terms, and both films depicted not only the wonders of the Green and Yampa Canyons, but the joys of running the river with Bus Hatch.[19]

Efforts by the Sierra Club, other groups such as the National Parks and Conservation Association and the Izzak Walton League, the *National Geographic* article, and Eggert's films, finally turned the tide of public opinion against the dam. In March 1956, after years of acrimonious debate, the hotly-disputed dams were finally withdrawn from legislation authorizing the Colorado River Storage Project,[20] and President Eisenhower signed the bill into law the next month. Even though supporters tried to resurrect the dam well into the 1960s, after 1956 it was essentially a dead issue. Echo Park and the Green and Yampa canyons were saved. No small thanks is due to Bus Hatch, for on his trips he quietly preached his gospel. He took pro-dam groups down the river as well, but it made no difference in the end.

This is not to say that Bus Hatch single-handedly defeated the Echo Park Dam; far from it, for it was a grass-roots effort that encompassed the Sierra Club, other conservation organizations, private individuals, well known authors, scholars, and scientists, and the behind-the-scenes opposition of the Congressional delegations from California, who wanted a dam closer to their state. But Bus was in the middle of the controversy for its entire duration, and was one of the very few people in Vernal to benefit from the defeat of the dam.

The decade following World War was an important one is Bus's life. Those ten years saw him go from a local contractor to a nationally known figure, from an uncertain living in the off-again on-again building trade to a booming business as a river outfitter. Through it all, Bus retained his sense of humor, his desire for of perfection, and his love of life. Now, with all the publicity generated by the Echo Park Dam controversy, the future looked bright for Bus and for Hatch River Expeditions. But first, another challenge awaited him, a challenge that would take him to the far corners of the earth.

e n d n o t e s

1 The property was later bought by A.K. Reynolds and his wife Ellen, who ran it for many years. Reynolds started his own river running company, Reynolds-Hallacy River Expeditions, with his brother-in-law Mike Hallacy. Using boats made from the plans for Norm Nevills's Cataract boats, they ran fishing, hunting, and photography trips on the upper Green from Green River, Wyoming, through Dinosaur National Monument. After Hallacy was drafted during the Korean War, Reynolds continued under the name Reynolds Expeditions, until construction started on Flaming Gorge Dam in 1956.

2 Don Hatch to Otis Marston, 11 January 1957.

3 "The 'Ugly Ducklings'," " by Don Hatch, *American Whitewater,* 1957. Within ten years, inflatables had all but replaced wooden boats for river running. The last company to use them commercially, until their revival as a novelty in the 1970s, was Mexican Hat Expeditions, the successor to Nevills Expedition, who used them until 1969.

4 Don Hatch interview, 10 March 1984.

5 Sources on the Echo Park Dam controversy are legion. For this book, I've used "Utah and the Echo Park Dam Controversy," by Susan Mae Neel, Masters Thesis, University of Utah, 1980. For Bus's feelings about the dam proposal, Don Hatch interview, 15 January 1988.

6 For many years, residents of Vernal tried to entice a railroad line into the Uinta Basin, with no success. The closest a rail line ever came was the Uintah Railway, built to carry Gilsonite from the mines south and east of Vernal in the early years of the 20th century. It came within 30 miles of Vernal, and plans were made to extend it so

that Vernal would have a connection with the Denver and Rio Grande Railroad in western Colorado, but they came to nothing.

7 "Dams will Enhance Monument Say Echo Park River Runners," *Vernal Express*, 15 September 1950. p. 1.

8 "Echo Park Lake," *Vernal Express*, 20 May 1954.

9 Don Hatch to Otis R. Marston, 11 January 1957. Marston Collection. The others were C.C. Manion, Don Howard, Leon Christensen, Grant Merrill, Bus Hatch, Otto Roach, Harry Ratliff, Frank Hatch, Gil Hunter, Sam Hatch, Bill Slaugh, Ken Kaye, George Andrews.

10 "Rolling down the river," *Salt Lake Tribune*, 31 May 1951.

11 Steve Bradley telephone interview, 25 May 1988.

12 "High Water Holiday," unpublished manuscript by John L. Conarroe, July 1957

13 IBID.

14 Mark Garff interview, 6 January 1988.

15 Tom Hatch interview, 15 January 1988.

16 "Children Run Utah River Rapids," *Los Angeles Times*, 30 August 1953. Martin Litton went on to become an ardent environmentalist and defender of the Colorado River, and founded his own river running company, Grand Canyon Dories.

17 "One More Dinosaur Myth Exposed," *Deseret News*, 12 May 1954.

18 Jack Breed, "Shooting Rapids in Dinosaur Country," *National Geographic*, March 1954. p. 363-392.

19 Eggert became good friends with Don Hatch in the course of making his Dinosaur films, and in 1955 and 1956, made a journey all the way down the Green and Colorado Rivers, to film them before the great dams at Flaming Gorge and Glen Canyon were built. The two films were *A Canyon Voyage* and *Danger River*. Eggert showed the films on the lecture circuit for many years. He also later became involved in many other conservation battles, including the creation of Canyonlands National Park, and the successful efforts to stop the construction of dams in the Grand Canyon.

The Search for Shangri-La

T WAS COLD at the bottom of the deep gorge, cold and gloomy. The sun
never got down into this chasm, and with the raging river pounding by, it
was a dank, depressing place. The canyon walls were bare of vegetation—
floods scoured the canyon each spring, so that nothing could live there.
Bus sat on the pontoon as it rocked in the strong current. The boat at least
seemed impatient to be back in the river, but Bus was in no hurry. He had
sent Don ahead to scout the rapid below, to see if it was even runnable. Don
asked him to come with him, but Bus had replied, "No, son, I'll trust your
judgement. You look at it, and we'll run it however you say." So Bus waited,
alone with his thoughts.

What had brought Bus Hatch of Vernal, Utah, to this remote corner of the
earth, near where the borders of Pakistan, India, and Russia meet? A river,
naturally; he was here to run the Indus River, a mighty torrent, one of the world's
major rivers. It had never even been attempted before, and the local people
swore that to try to float it, no matter what the equipment and skills, was sheer
suicide. Bus had already run all of the canyons of the Colorado, the Green, the
Snake, and the Salmon—the major whitewater streams in the western United
States. His reputation as the premier fast-water man in the country was already
assured, although he didn't really care for such false honors.

It all began with the same man who had introduced Bus to the Sierra Club
at the start of the Echo Park Dam controversy, Steve Bradley. While skiing at
Stowe, in Vermont, Bradley had met Lowell Thomas, the radio personality

and documentary film maker. Thomas had almost run over Bradley's wife on the ski slope, and came back to apologize. They became "occasional" friends after that, and kept in touch. One day Bradley got a call from Thomas, who asked him to help him with his latest Cinerama film project. Thomas was a leader in the development of the new Cinerama technology, which used a special camera with three lenses and a stereo soundtrack to create a film that surrounded the viewer.

Thomas had already made several travel and adventure films. For his next project, he wanted to take his cameras and crew to Nepal to film the coronation of the crown prince. Then two actors, playing recently discharged airmen in the U.S. Air Force, would begin a "search for shangri-la," that would take them through India, Pakistan, and Afghanistan. Thomas's cameras would film this journey. A part of their search would include a journey down the Indus River. Thomas knew that Bradley was a kayaker, and he planned to have Steve kayak the river while the Cinerama camera filmed the dramatic whitewater voyage.[1]

Thomas sent Steve to Pakistan, to reconnoiter the headwaters of the Indus. The area was as remote as any on earth, and only twenty-five miles from the border of the Soviet Union. Furthermore, it was at the center of a tense stand-off between India and Pakistan over possession of Kashmir. Still, Bradley agreed to go. He traveled to Karachi by air, then flew to Rawalpindi, far in the interior, and further still to Skardu, near the Indian border. This provincial capitol was accessible only by air, or a two-week journey over the ancient trail by camel train. Bradley flew into Skardu in a DC-3 and began his search for a stretch of the river that was both photogenic and runnable.

The script called for scenes showing the kayak negotiating rapids with the towering mountains of the Karakoram in the background, but such settings were not to be found. In most of the gorges, the walls were too steep to allow for a view of the surrounding mountains. In those few places where both conditions were met, the rapids were completely unrunnable. Finally, though, after several weeks of searching, Bradley found a 30-mile stretch of the Indus above Skardu that could at least be run, but not in a kayak. The Indus carried over four times the water of the Colorado at flood stage, or about 500,000 second-feet. Bradley was a skilled kayaker, but he realized that this river called for something better suited to big-water rapids.

Back in Rawalpindi, Bradley met with Thomas' director, Otto Lang, who was a veteran motion picture director. Lang told him that since they were behind schedule, they would begin filming the river running sequence immediately with the boats they had already purchased. Bradley demanded to see the boats, and try them out in a swimming pool with sandbags to simulate the weight of the Cinerama camera and battery packs. When they unpacked the boats, it was immediately obvious that whoever had sold them to Lowell Thomas had no idea of what they were going to be used for. The boats were lightweight survival rafts, totally inadequate to even float the Indus, let alone run the rapids with camera and crew aboard. Bradley cabled Thomas back in New York, and told him that if they wanted to film this part of the movie, they would need the best boats and the most experienced rivermen around—call Bus Hatch.

Thomas called Bus, then in Vernal, one day in the early summer of 1956, and explained the situation to him. "Bus, I want you and your son Don to go to Pakistan and run the Indus River," Thomas said. "It's never been run, and all that've attempted it have been drowned," he warned. Bus didn't hesitate; "We'll try it." At the time, Don was just starting into the Grand Canyon on the last leg of a movie trip with Charles Eggert. Bus arranged for Smuss Allen, one of their best boatmen, to hike into Phantom Ranch and take over for Don. He would then hike out and catch a plane. Bus arranged for one of their 27-foot pontoons and a ten-man raft to be flown to New York, and thence to Karachi. He planned to use the pontoon for the camera boat, and the ten-man raft for the action sequences.

Bus later said that he had never even heard of Pakistan—"It was all India when I went to school," he later commented.[2] Within a few weeks, he found himself in Rawalpindi, awaiting a flight to Skardu. Staying at Flashman's Hotel, Bus "learned fast and furious," about how things were done in Pakistan. In the dining room, for instance, each guest had his own waiter. Bus's was eager to bring him anything he wanted, but there wasn't much that Bus did want. His first meal was of a rice cake cooked with fish, but when he tried it he found that it was rancid. Bus was warned not to eat the fresh vegetables, as they would give him dysentery. "What the hell," he said, "you get it anyway." He finally convinced the waiter that he wanted his rice without the curry sauce that covered every dish, so that he could at least have something filling to eat.

When the weather finally cleared, Bus boarded a DC-3 that was stripped of everything but its aluminum bucket seats so that it could carry the boats and motors. Just as he was getting ready to go, here came Don and the production manager, Ed Evans, who had just arrived in Rawalpindi. They told him to go on ahead, and they would be on the next plane in the morning. The mountains were so high that the plane had to fly through the canyons. Bus thought that the pilot was flying awfully close to the canyon wall, but when he looked out the window on the other side of the plane, the other canyon wall was just as close. When they finally landed at the Northern Scouts Army airfield in Skardu, Bus asked about the crumpled mass of metal at the end of the field. That was a DC-3 a few weeks ago, he was told—another flight was three weeks overdue. After a deep breath, he found a hotel and settled down to wait for the rest of the crew.

It was a long wait, for the weather closed in and it was two weeks before the next flight could bring in his son Don or any of the Cinerama crew. Staying at the guest house of the provincial governor's palace, Bus was fortunate enough to meet a Captain Alim, an English-speaking doctor in the Northern Scouts Army. Captain Alim and Bus became friends, and the captain became Bus's mentor, protector and contact for his dealings with the local population. He supplied Bus with a jeep and a driver, so that he could at least scout from the shore the stretch of river they were to run. There were some terrific rapids, but as Bus said, "the worst danger was in the jeep, on the trail." The good captain took Bus under his wing and taught him what to eat. Beef was sacred, pork was taboo, and the little goats that passed for lamb smelled so bad that he couldn't stand to eat them. For two weeks he lived on rice, minus the curry sauce that they insisted on adding, and an occasional egg. Nor were his problems all dietary, as he found when he tried to plug in his electric razor. There was a flash of sparks, and he quickly jerked the plug from the wall. Pakistan, it seemed, was on 220 current, while the U.S. was on 110-volt current. Undeterred, Bus split the cord, plugged one end into the outlet, wired the other to the faucet on the sink, and had his shave.

Exasperated, Bus sent out a telegram saying that unless the rest of the crew came in, so that they could get going on the filming, he was coming out, although it was a two-week walk over mountain trails to Rawalpindi. As it was, he lost fifteen pounds during his two-week stay. Finally Don and Otto Lang arrived. The governor of the province invited them all to a banquet in honor of the occasion. Their first question to Bus was "What do we eat? What do we eat?" "To hell with you," Bus replied, "I had to find out for myself, when you left me here two weeks alone. You find out." So Lang and Don followed Bus around at the banquet, and when he started eating a lamb stew, they dove in "like pigs at a trough."

All together at last, they were ready for a trial run of boats and equipment. Following Steve Bradley's recommendation, they hauled one of their boats upriver to a place about thirty miles above Skardu, where it was carried down from the trail by a gang of native bearers. The run back down to Skardu was

an eye-opener. The rapids were bigger than anything on the Colorado, and there was four times as much water. The current ran about ten miles an hour, and the water, from melting glaciers, was icy. Don ran the motors, while Bus worked the oars. Finally, they came to a calm stretch where they could get their breath. As Don later wrote, however, that was small comfort:

> A calm stretch of river in a granite canyon of this sort indicated only one thing to us; a bad rapid was immediately below, and had back up the water on which we now floated.[3]

When Don walked downstream to scout the rapid, his heart fell. The whole river seemed to disappear, and all he could see below were clouds of spray. The entire force of the current poured against a sheer cliff on the right, pushing the water to the left and creating a huge swirling eddy. To make it worse, right at

The Story of Bus Hatch

the head of the rapid was a house-sized boulder, splitting the current in two, further narrowing the choices of where to run. In an article published the next year, Don described what happened next:

> We ran according to plan, but were shocked on our approach to find the waves much bigger than anticipated and far more rugged. There was nothing to do but grit our teeth in defiance—one of us did the cussing, the others prayed. Camel hair ropes were tied across the boat; we gripped them desperately for support and I "poured the coal" to the motor. To say we felt like flies on our way to the sewer would be putting it mildly. The pontoon hit the first hole and the sides collapsed until they touched. One "cooley" lay quivering in the bottom. Another gripped iron rings in the nose of the boat. After that first hole no one was standing. Water had flattened us all. Our director, Otto Lang, was hit by water and knocked across my lap. We both nearly went out of the boat.... The boat was nearly full of water as it charged toward the cliff below. A huge water cushion had been built up in front of us, and had it not been for this, our boat would have dashed headlong against the cliff. As it was we slithered against the cliff in a gentle fashion, hung for a moment, and floated off to the left.[4]

Also along was Captain Alim, who had been on many mountain-climbing expeditions and wanted to see the river. The captain held on better than Lang. The thirty-mile trip only took them four hours.

Although the rapids were fierce, once Bus and Don were on the water the old instincts took over and they were able to make good runs of all of the rapids. Steve Bradley had made a detailed map of this section, which helped them make their way downriver without any more problems. On shore in Skardu, Bus and Don felt that they could run this section with the camera and crew aboard. Lang, however, felt differently. "I was merely a wide-eyed passenger," he later wrote, "and have rarely witnessed such a cataclysmic force of nature, only comparable to being swept away by an avalanche." Lang had been badly shaken by the experience, and decided that they would have to find another stretch to film.[5]

At his insistence, they moved over to the Gilgit River, a tributary of the Indus not very far downstream. The new plan was to put the boats into the Gilgit, then film them all the way down to the confluence with the Indus. They made their final preparations in the village of Gilgit. The morning of the launch, the boats were all rigged, the motors were purring, the Cinerama

camera mounted and ready, and the crew ready to go, when suddenly a boy ran up and said the police were coming for them. The ruler of the province, a stately old man with a gold-headed cane, soon appeared, followed by the chief of police. "We have no authority to stop you," he announced to Bus, "but I beg you not to try the river. Everyone who has tried it before has been lost, and you surely will too." "We tried a lot of rivers that were bad," Bus told him, "and we came halfway around the world to run this one."

The official, not to be easily dissuaded, offered to take them personally to show them the rapids. "Shut off the motors, boys, we'll try it in the morning," Bus said. "He just about walked me and Don to death," Bus later remembered, as they hiked along the trail to look at the river. With his gold-headed cane, the chief would point out the rapids, saying surely they couldn't run that

When there's no roads and no winch trucks

one. Each time, to the chief's disappointment, Bus told him "No, we've ru[n] worse than that." Finally, the official's conscience was assuaged, and the nex[t] morning they took off down the river.

The film in the Cinerama camera lasted only eleven minutes, and it too[k] two technicians forty minutes to change the film. So every half hour or s[o] they had to find a place to land so they could change film. The current was s[o] strong that Bus had to keep the motor running to keep the boat from bein[g] swept away. At one such stop the assistant cameramen, Jack Priestly, jumpe[d] from the boat and began climbing up the side of the mountain. When Bu[s] called to him to come back, he refused, saying that he had sworn if he ever go[t] his feet on solid ground, under no circumstances would he would get back i[n] the boat. Although he was on the opposite side of the river from the trail, Bu[s] couldn't talk him into getting back in the boat, so they left him. At the nex[t] stop, Bus made sure he stopped on the same side of the river. Sure enough, her[e] came Priestly, who had worked his way along the river bank. Bus convince[d] him to get back in the boat, by promising him that as soon as they got nea[r] a village, he would drop him off, which they did. After he had calmed dow[n] Priestly later rejoined the crew.

Stopped for a rest, Bus tied the boat up tight so that the swift curren[t] couldn't work it loose. When they went back down to the river, he found tha[t] the boat had been moved. "Evil spirits," the native workers said, pleading wit[h] Bus to give up the trip lest they all be drowned. It was a little disconcertin[g] Bus later commented, to have men pleading for their lives every night an[d] have to run the river every day. But run the river they did, shooting thousand[s] of feet of film, facing rapids that had never been run and running them as [a] matter of course. Some of the film was sent out to new York for developin[g] and word came back that the shots were turning out perfectly. As the day[s]

Riverma[n]

went on, Bus began to feel like the river was home once again.

At length, they had the film "in the can," and were ready to call it done. Bus climbed out to the trail, and arranged for the truck to meet them the next day to carry crew and equipment back to Gilgit. They had been completely successful both in running the river and in filming. The next morning, however, Lang came to Bus and said that he wanted to get one more action sequence. Towering over their camp was Nanga Parbat, known among mountaineers as the "killer mountain." As of 1956, almost forty mountain climbers had died attempting to reach its snow-clad summit. Lang wanted to film a scene with the "killer mountain in the background. Reluctantly, Bus agreed.

Lang's idea was for Don to run a rapid just below their camp in the ten-man raft, while Bus followed in the camera boat. Just as they were getting ready to push off, one of the actors, Jim Parker, jumped on the boat and asked if he could go along. Parker was not one of the boat crew, and they had no life jackets to spare, but Bus let him stay on the boat. He was from Colorado, a good friend of Steve Bradley. An outdoorsman and athlete, Parker was also an excellent swimmer. Although he hadn't been in any of the river sequences, Parker was in love with the beauty of the region. Just the night before, as they sat around the campfire, he had told Bus that he loved Pakistan so much that he would like to spend the rest of his life there.

Bus was at the oars, with Otto Lang and Dusty Wallace, one of the production crew, at the motors. Neither one had ever run a boat before, so they were depending on Bus for directions. Bus later told what happened next:

> We were getting close into the rapid, and it looked like we were going to plow Don under. I shouted "get out of there, get out quick Don, get out to the left." Don said "I got one bad oar, Dad,"—he had a third oar, and he switched oars, and he was ducking out to the left. But to keep from running over him, I signaled my motors to turn our boat to the left. They turned to the left, Don got clear, and before we could get the big boat back around straight, we were into the rapids, on an angle. And it came over just as easy as anything. It rolled very slowly, it seemed to me, and there I was upside down, under the boat, with a rope half-hitched right above the knee.

"It was the worst churning I ever got," Bus said, but by "curling up like a shrimp," he was able to get his breath every time the boat rose over a wave. He finally worked his leg free, but not before it was badly wrenched. Bus had been out of boats before, and knew instinctively what to do. If it had been any of the others, they probably would have drowned. When he got out from under the boat, the first person he saw was Jack Priestly, who was trying to climb onto the boat and screaming "What do I do, what do I do?" Bus had him hold onto a d-ring, and worked his way around to see where the rest of the crew was. The boat finally drifted into an eddy; when Bus let go to swim to shore, he discovered his life jacket had been torn off in the violent water. He made it to shore anyway, and when the pontoon came near, he waded out and pulled it in:

> This big Dusty Wallace was ashore, and he came out and helped me get the boat in, and tied. And there was what was left of my crew. Pete Passos, the Greek was missing, Jim Parker was missing, Otto Lang, who's a very tough man, he's a rigid, rugged character, he was sitting on a rock, his head in his hands, saying "Poor Don, poor Don." "My God, Otto [Bus said] shut up. Don's a good boatman, and he had a boat under him the last I saw him." "Thank God you're here, Bus," [Lang replied]. I looked around, there was one vomiting, and one was wringing his hands. The calm one of the lot was this big Dusty Wallace. I said "Dusty, I was under there. Get under [the boat] and see if Parker or Passos are under there. So he held the ring and felt with his feet, and says "Nobody under there, including the camera."

While the others hiked downstream to see if they could find what had happened to Don or the two missing men, Bus tied the boat more securely. The camera had been secured to the boat by a heavy nylon strap and chains. The chains, however, had been bought in Pakistan, and they were hand-forged. When the boat rolled, the links had broken, and the weight of the camera had torn the d-ring and nylon strap right off the boat. "It was still purring nicely," Bus commented, when it went under.

Don, who had made it through the rapid, saw gas cans and oars come floating by, and pulled into an eddy to see what had happened. He picked up Pete Passos, and got to shore. There was no sign of Jim Parker. Once all the crew got back together, they realized they had to get out of the canyon while Bus could still walk—his leg was almost dislocated by the force of the current while he was under the boat, and he knew that once it started to swell from the injury, he wouldn't be able to walk. The next day, some of the crew went to look in a big eddy just downstream, to see if there was any trace of Parker. All they found was some floating debris and Bus's lifejacket. An expensive model from Abercrombie and Fitch, it had ripped right up the back and come off over his head. Although the local villagers searched for some time, there was no trace of Jim Parker. He was never seen again. He had wanted to spend the rest of his life in Pakistan, and he had gotten his wish. What had been a triumph had turned to tragedy.

That was the end of the filming, but not their troubles. Bus's leg was so twisted that he couldn't walk, and Don had contracted typhoid. They spent two weeks in the hospital in Rawalpindi before either one of them could travel. Finally, they packed up the equipment and headed home. Since they were just about exactly half-way around the world from Salt Lake City, they continued on across the Pacific, flying all the way around the world. They arrived back in the U.S. in August, 1956. In San Francisco, Bus asked the ticket agent to change his ticket from New York to Salt Lake City, expecting to get a refund. But instead, the agent told him that it would be an extra $30. "I know I'm a country hick and I look it, but I'm not that dumb," Bus said, but the clerk explained that the ticket was a round-the-world rate. To change it would cost extra. Bus didn't change his ticket, but he got off in Salt Lake City anyway. He was weary of traveling, and just wanted to get home.

Bus soon settled back into his routines of building, hunting and fishing, and running rivers. But Lowell Thomas wasn't through with the Hatches. He had Don take Otto Lang and the Cinerama crew down the Grand Canyon in one of the pontoons so that they could get some more rapid footage to round out the picture. To substitute for the Pakistani crewmen, Land hired local Navajo Indians and dressed them in Pakistani robes and turbans. Then Thomas flew both Bus and Don back to New York the next summer, so they could be there for the film's premier. For the opening of the film, now re-titled *Search for Paradise*, Thomas planned what would today be called a media event. He had the boat flown from Vernal to New York on an Air Force cargo plane— Thomas had connections as well as money. The boat was run up and down the East River; instead of Pakistanis pleading for their lives, the crew consisted of the mayor of New York, Lowell Thomas and other dignitaries, and several young glamour girls in bathing suits. At the premier itself, the movie-goers— all invited guests—had to wear life jackets, and at particularly exciting scenes water was sprayed from the balcony onto the screaming audience. Although the film didn't get very good reviews from the critics, it was a hit with most audiences around the country and played for years. The river sequences were considered the best part of the film by reviewers and the public alike.

On the basis of their exploits, both Bus and Don were awarded memberships in the prestigious Explorers Club. They appeared on the Arthur Godfrey radio program, and were the toast of New York for a brief flurry of publicity. Back home in Salt Lake, Don was often asked to give slide shows about the journey. The story appeared in *Life*, the *New Yorker*, and other national publications. Once again, Bus and Hatch River Expeditions were national figures.

But something was subtly changed in Bus. Although he never really said anything about it, the loss of Jim Parker had affected him deeply. No one had ever even been injured seriously while he was in charge of a boat, on any of his trips. Now a man had died, and even though it hadn't been his decision to make that last run, Bus felt responsible. Perhaps that had something to do with an incident on one of his commercial trips not too long after they returned from the Indus. Bus was taking a party of tourists down the Green, when an elderly woman fell out of one of the other boats in a rapid in Split Mountain Canyon. Even though he had always said that he would never do it, Bus dove into the swollen river and pulled the woman to shore. He said later that he realized at once that the woman couldn't swim well enough to stay afloat in the turbulent water. Bus got a lot of water in his lungs, and felt the effects for some time after that. But the woman was saved. Perhaps Bus was remembering that day in the gloomy gorges of the Indus, when against his better judgment he had allowed a man without a life jacket to ride on his boat.

endnotes

1   Bus Hatch interview, 1962; Don Hatch interview, 15 January 1988; Lowell Thomas, *So Long Until Tomorrow: From Quaker Hill to Kathmandu*, (William Morrow Co., 1977). p. 232-236.

2   Unless otherwise noted, all quotes in this chapter are from the Bus Hatch interview, 1962.

3 "Indus River Adventure," unpublished manuscript by Don Hatch.

4 "Adventure on the Indus," by Don Hatch. *American Whitewater*, Spring 1957. p. 5-7.

5   *So Long Until Tomorrow: From Quaker Hill to Kathmandu*. Lowell Thomas. (New York : William Morrow and Co., 1977). p. 234.

Looks Like An Oar Job, Boys

B Y THE MIDDLE of the 1950s, the controversy about the Echo Park Dam had finally begun to die down.[1] About the only person in Vernal who had directly benefited from all the publicity was Bus Hatch. During the debate, his river business had grown to the point that for the first time, he was working at that as much as at his usual work, contracting. Although the exploits on the Indus didn't attract as much attention in Vernal as the dam controversy, the Indus trip and the association with Lowell Thomas still served to introduce Bus and the river to a wider clientele. Whereas most of the river customers had up to this time come from California and the west, now individuals and groups from the east coast began to call on Bus for trips down the Green and Colorado.

The days of Bus running trips by himself, and going on every trip, were long over, and few of his old partners were running the river anymore. Cap Mowrey had settled into a good business in Vernal, buying houses, then fixing them up and selling them. Alt was living in Boulder, Colorado, where he managed the J.C. Penney store. Tom quit the river after his near-fatal accident in 1935, and had since moved to Alaska. Frank Swain still ran the river on occasion, but rarely with Bus. Frank was settled in Copperton, Utah, where he was the security officer for the mining company.[2] Another of the pioneers of the 1930s, Roy DeSpain, still ran his own boats, taking groups of Boy Scouts from Provo or Springville down the Yampa or the Green.[3] Now and then Bus

would give him a call, asking him to help out with a Sierra Club trip or other large group.

But by this time, Bus had other members of his family to turn to. All of his sons helped out on trips, even before they were big enough to row boats. Don chose teaching as a career, so he could take the summers off and run the river. After he graduated from the University of Utah in 1950, he was on the Green or the Middle Fork or the Grand Canyon every summer. Frank and Ted,[4] the next-youngest and the youngest sons, would hike up into the lower end of Split Mountain Canyon when they knew their dad was coming off the river with a group of passengers. While they waited, they would swim through Inglesby Rapid, sometimes several times—much to their mother's dismay. When the boats showed up, they would ride down, and then help unload and de-rig the big pontoons. By the time he was a teenager Ted was running trips on his own, and later, for the same reason as Don, became a teacher.

Bus was as hard on his sons as he was on anyone else who worked for him—perhaps even more so. He was still very much the perfectionist, and had lost none of his quick temper. He would chew out his sons just like he would anyone else whom he felt hadn't measured up, but as soon as he had made his point—i.e., you made a mistake, and don't do it again—he was back to his old self. Ted remembered taking a trip on the Yampa with Bus, when he was only about nine years old. He was running a motor on a wooden boat, with Bus sitting at the oars. As they approached the head of Big Joe Rapid, Bus told Ted to go to the left. Ted, used to oars, turned the handle to the left instead, sending the boat to the right and directly into a big hole at the top of the rapid.

So the boat turned the wrong way and I went into the worst hole. It was high water, in the spring. It filled that boat with water, and it started to actually sink. Dad jumped and grabbed the oars—the motor was sputtering, you know. He told me to head for shore, the motor was barely [going]. He grabbed those oars and started to row and help me, and as we went in the boat went under, and we settled in the sand. We were sitting there about to our armpits in the water, but we made it. He says "Bail, bail!" and I said "It's coming over the sides!" He looked, and then he cussed me. I'd really screwed up, and as a riverman, you don't do that. He let me know, that's not where you run Big Joe.[5]

Bus also recruited his first grandson, Tom, who was Gus's oldest son. Tom used to follow his granddad around, begging him to take him along on river trips. At first he went as a camp helper, gathering firewood, tending the fires, doing any chore, just to get to go on the trip. When he was thirteen, he figured he was old enough to run a boat, and approached Bus about it.

Bus asked me if I could run that boat. I said "Well, I think so," and he lit right in the middle of me—there was no mercy. He said "Jesus Christ, son, can you or can't you?" Just that quick I said "Yes, I can." "That's all I wanted to know," [Bus replied]. "I'll put you on the river in the morning."[6]

It was Tom who would later comment that Bus must have been quite religious, for he prefaced every remark with "Jesus Christ!" Besides Tom, Don's sons Craig and Barry also worked for Bus—Craig ran trips alone when he was only fourteen years old. But even with four sons, and his grandson, and an occasional hand from old friends such as Roy DeSpain, Bus still had more business than he could handle. To help out, at first he hired local boys from Vernal, friends of his sons, or distant relatives. Glade Ross, George Wilkins, Johnny Caldwell, and Jesse Burton were among the many who went to work for Bus during the 1950s. His method of hiring was casual. He would take the prospective boatman along on a trip as a swamper, or camp helper. One trip was enough for Bus to make up his mind. If Bus liked him, he was hired. If not, Bus thanked him politely and sent him on his way. Later, after he developed a cadre of men he trusted, Bus would send the new hand out on a training trip with one of his senior boatmen. If the boatman thought he could make a river runner out of the swamper, that was good enough for Bus. The opposite also applied.

George Wilkins, a native of Vernal, still remembers his first trip with Bus. It was 1957, when George was fifteen years old. The spring flood was exceptionally high on the Green and the Colorado that year—the combined rivers contained over 100,000 second-feet of water. The trip scheduled was Cataract Canyon, one of the worst stretches of the Colorado. Glade Ross, another Vernal teenager but already one of Bus's best boatman, had run a trip down Cataract shortly before, and had capsized one of the big pontoons. As they rolled the boats out to pump them up, one of them came off the truck upside down. Before they turned it over, Glade took a can of orange spray paint and wrote "HATCH" on the bottom of the boat. When George asked him what he was doing, Glade replied, "I flipped last month—this time, when we go over I want them to know who they are looking for."

By the time they had gotten the boats out and blown up, Bus had had second thoughts about running such a rough stretch of canyon when the water was so high. It was a regular commercial group—mostly adults, but there were some older people and some children. One of the passengers challenged Bus, accusing him of being afraid to run Cataract. Bus bristled. "The little banty rooster [Bus] jumped in the boat and said 'I'm sixty years old, and I've lived a full life. If I die tomorrow, I'll be happy. How about you and your wife and kids? 'Cause I'm not afraid to take you through there.'" The passenger backed down, and they decided to drive on down to Mexican Hat, Utah, and run the San Juan River instead.[7]

While on the San Juan, a much easier river, George was running the motor on the boat. Bus, in the front of the boat, told Wilkins to follow his arm signals: if Bus pointed right, it meant to go right; if he held his hand straight up, to go straight, and so on.

> [Bus] was up in the front of the boat talking to people, and he started waving his arms. His right arm, then his left arm, then he'd give me the pointer. Well Bus, if you tied his hands behind his back, couldn't say a word. And so he was talking to these people, and he would, I thought, give me directions to the right or the left, and I hit about six rocks. And Bus come back and he said "Jesus Christ son-of-a-bitch, son, what's the matter?" I said "Well, I could see the rock over there, but I thought you wanted me to go over that

way, I thought maybe you had seen something over on the other side. He said "Oh, Jesus Christ son-of-a-bitch, son, just run the boat, and forget what I told you." And that was my training trip.[8]

Bus sent young Wilkins out the next week with a full load of passengers, on a trip down the Yampa, and George worked for Hatch River Expeditions until after Bus's death.

As word got around about Hatch River Expeditions, Bus would hire others who came to him looking for a good summer job. Mark Garff was a young man from Salt Lake City who got his start on the river when he went on a Boy Scout trip down Glen Canyon with the famous Moki-Mac Ellingson in 1950. A few years later, he went down the Yampa with another scout group, and met Bus at Box Elder campground. Mark asked Bus for a job, and Bus just laughed and said "You boys from Salt Lake can't handle this kind of work." Garff persisted, and finally talked Bus into giving him a try, on a Sierra Club trip down Lodore. Mark was at the front set of oars on a pontoon. After a few days, he realized that Bus wasn't rowing, just sitting at the back set giving commands and laughing. Mark laughed too, and he was part of the family. Mark Garff is another who worked for Bus every summer while obtaining college and graduate degrees, and helped out whenever he could thereafter. There were many others—some would stay for just a season or two; others would stay for life. Among the former group were local youths such as Earl Staley, a member of the Island Park family that owned the Ruple ranch, and Bill Slaugh, a Vernal car salesman who just liked to go down the river. Two brothers from Salt Lake City, Bruce and Clarke Lium, worked for Hatch off and on for years. Clarke started with Sierra Club trips in 1953, and was supposed to accompany the 1955 Hatch-Eggert filming trip. When he was unable to make it, his brother Bruce took over. More out of the ordinary were pioneer kayakers Walter Kirschbaum and Roger Paris. Kirschbaum, a German veteran of World War II, had learned "wildwasser" (wild water) kayaking in Germany before the war, and after his release from a Russian prison camp in 1955, came to the U.S., where he won a number of kayaking championships. Roger Paris, from France, likewise was an established kayaking expert, and winner of many races in Europe and America. He met Don Hatch on a Sierra Club trip on the Yampa, and went to work for Bus in 1957. Even though both were recognized expert kayakers, both also just liked to be on the river, so they worked for Bus at one time or another. Those who stayed for longer included a cowboy from up around Browns Park, Jesse Burton. Jesse—always known as Shorty, even though he tall and lanky—started out working for Bus when he was just a teenager, but soon became one of Bus's most trusted boatmen. He was especially known for his skills as a camp cook, and became famous on the river for producing wonderful pies.[9]

Whether they worked for a single trip or for years, virtually all boatmen came away with wonderful memories of Bus. One reason so many boatmen, from so many walks of life, remained so fiercely loyal to Bus can be explained with one word—family. Anyone who went to work for Bus was immediately accepted as part of the family, and treated just like his own sons. George Wilkins echoed everyone's sentiments:

> That's one thing about Bus Hatch; you work for him, the word "son" meant exactly what it means. You needed a car, they had 'em. Gas it up. If you needed some money, if you had money coming, he'd pay you all the money you had coming and whatever you figured you needed extra. It was just that way, whatever you needed. When you worked for him, it was like family.

But being a part of Bus's extended family went both ways. His quick temper and exacting standards were not for everyone. If a boatman worked hard and

fast, and didn't make the same mistake twice, he got along with Bus just fine. But if a new hand kept making mistakes, or shirked his duties, watch out. As his grandson Tom remembers, "If you were doing a man's job you took a man's chewing, and he wasn't above chewing you out. But if you worked hard and tried and did your best, he didn't expect more than that. One minute you were a knucklehead, the next he would pat you on the back and you were his best hand." Everyone agreed that once you learned about his temper, and you learned very quickly, you got along just fine. If a man didn't, he didn't last.

On a typical trip with Bus in the 1950s, the boatmen would show up at the Hatch yard on 4th East Street in Vernal, early on the day before the passengers were scheduled to arrive. Some were sent over to Ashton's store to buy the food for the trip—Ralph Ashton would often open his store up on Sunday or at night so that Bus's crew could get supplies. Once the boats, food boxes, and duffle were loaded onto the old double axle trailer, the boatmen would head for Lily Park or Gates of Lodore, to inflate and rig the boats and get them loaded with the gear. Whoever was standing around the yard, even if they weren't scheduled to work, would often get recruited on the spot and sent out with the crew, to help rig the boats and then drive the old Chevrolet panel truck back to town. The next day, the passengers would arrive early in the morning at the boat yard, board the old schoolbus, and be driven out to the launch site. There were assigned to a boat and given a few safety instructions. After they were all loaded, they would shove off.

Bus almost always used the big pontoons for large groups, because they were safer and you could get more people on each one, thus cutting down on overhead. In Dinosaur, they used two sets of oars per boat. When they came to rapids, the passengers would usually get off the boat and walk around. The boatmen would double up on the oars, trading off back or front set of oars depending on whose boat it was. Bus, Don, or Ted always ran first. The man in the back was in charge, and would call commands to the front oarsman—Bus was no exception to this, and often took his turn at the front oars. Manhandling one of the big 28-foot pontoons down a narrow river was no easy job, even in those pre-dam flows. A fully loaded pontoon, with ten or twelve passengers, all their gear and a share of the cooking utensils and food could weigh several tons.[10]

Later, when Bus began running Cataract Canyon and the Grand Canyon regularly, they used outboard motors. At first they just hung the motor off the back of the boat, an arrangement called a "tail-dragger." But outboards in those days were not sealed, and if water came up over the motor it would drown it out, necessitating a quick jump to the oars. Ted Hatch remembered sitting around at night, drying spark plugs so they would be ready for the next day. The motor was also precariously exposed in rocky rapids, as was the boatman; being out at the end of twenty-seven feet of flexible rubber meant that as the boat went over waves, the was a real chance of him getting launched into the air as the stern of the boat crested the wave.[11] Bus was constantly experimenting,

tinkering with the rigging of his boats, and what a boatman went out with on one trip might bear no resemblance to what kind of equipment he used on his next.

Bus had a real love-hate relationship with outboard motors. On the one hand, they were a way to speed things up, and Bus lived his whole life in a hurry. On the other, he was just old-fashioned enough not to trust them. Don Hatch recalled one time when they were all loaded and ready to shove off. Bus jumped into the boat, started the motor, and revved it up. However, he had forgotten to take the motor out of neutral, so it just raced without moving the boat. Bus twisted the throttle several times with no result, and finally dropped the handle in disgust, thinking the motor was broken. He looked at Don and the passengers and said, "Well, looks like an oar job, boys."

Once they got to camp, the boatman's work had just begun. If it was a Sierra Club trip that brought their own cooks and commissary, it wasn't quite as much work. But on most trips, the boatmen then turned into cooks. With a small group, sometimes they would cut cards to see who cooked, who washed dishes, who gathered firewood. With a big group, everyone pitched in. Bus insisted that the food be the best they could have, and that everyone get as much as they wanted. "I don't want you to bring anybody off a trip hungry," he would tell his crews, and many former passengers remember the elaborate dutch-oven meals as the high point of the trip. The swampers (trainee boatmen) and willing passengers gathered firewood and tended the fires, while the boatmen prepared the dinner. Bus, in the meantime, would be doing what he loved best—telling stories to the passengers. After dinner, while the satiated passengers went for a hike or relaxed, the crew cleaned up, got the next morning's breakfast ready, secured the foodboxes against ravens and squirrels, had a drink or two by themselves, and finally went to bed.

Drinking was very much a part of the tradition of the West, and Bus was no exception. He and his pards had long carried a jug of moonshine along to warm them up on chilly nights, and this tradition carried over onto the commercial trips of the 1950s. The crew was usually up by 4 A.M., and worked hard all day, rowing, taking care of passengers, loading and unloading the big boats. If you did your job and didn't complain, then nobody minded if you had a drink or even got drunk before bed. You worked hard, you played hard, and when you drank, you drank hard. Bus enjoyed it as much as the next person, but he never let it affect his judgment on the river. One former boatman remembers that one of his duties was to get up before the passengers and get the breakfast fire going. Bus, who was sleeping nearby, called him over one day and said "Son, bring me about two fingers of whiskey in this cup." He downed it at a gulp, and got up to face the day. When the passengers got up, Bus was standing there fixing eggs like he had been up for hours.[12] Other river runners were less inclined to drink on the river; Norm Nevills, for instance, was a teetotaler who didn't drink at all and didn't allow alcohol on his trips, but neither Bus nor any of his crew ever felt they had to apologize for having a toddy or two on a cold morning.

If the trip was on the Green or the Yampa, often the trucks would meet the party at Island Park and off-load the camp gear, to be taken back to the yard in Vernal. The boats were then taken through with just the passengers aboard, making for an easier ride through the rapids of Split Mountain. At the end of Split Mountain Canyon, the passengers would disperse to their cars, already shuttled over to the parking lot. The boatmen and whoever was rounded up among the other crew at the yard would de-rig, deflate, and load the rolled boats, a process one former crew member likened to "handling a dead elephant." Food boxes, coolers, and whatever was left went on next, and then the weary crew would head back into town. Although they were supposed to get a couple of days off in town, as often as not, the crew went right back out with another group the next day. Tom Hatch remembered spending thirty-two consecutive days on the river, in town only long enough to replenish the food boxes.

For the residents of Vernal, Bus and his boat crews were a different breed altogether. George Wilkins remembers that in all the years he worked for Hatch,

he only took one passenger from Vernal down the river, and for their part, the boatmen seldom showed up in town. Glade Ross, for instance, was taken for a ghost when he returned to Vernal from a long Grand Canyon trip one year. The other boatmen had told anyone who asked about Glade's whereabouts that he had drowned in the Colorado. When they were in town, they dressed in their standard uniform of tennis shoes and Levi jackets with no sleeves, unlike the locals' cowboy boots and jeans. They were always tanned, even in the spring, from running trips in Arizona during the early part of the river season.

Bus paid his crews $20 per day on the river, good wages at the time. There was no place to spend it in Lodore or the Yampa, and many of them lived for free in bunkhouses at the boat yard, so the boatmen usually had money in their pockets. Naturally, they were irresistible to the local girls, and just as naturally were intensely disliked by the other young men in town. But problems were rare, and his boatmen never had time to get into trouble anyway. After a day or two, Bus would call and say "There's a trip going out tomorrow, and we need a hand. Get down here." And they were off again, down the Grand Canyon, or Lodore, or the Middle Fork.

During the 1950s, Bus began to re-visit scenes of his earlier times on the river. Dr. Frazier, Frank Swain and others had gone down the Middle Fork in the late '30s and '40s, but Bus had not been with them. In 1954 he went back up to Idaho, to run the Salmon River for the first time in almost twenty years. He took a party from Colorado that included several of the Coors heirs, and his friend Darcey Brown. The Coors group brought more duffle than any of them had ever seen, and the 10-man rafts were piled high with gear and supplies. Bus rowed one boat, and Mark Garff was the boatman on the other. Mark had never been on the Salmon, and thought nothing of it when Bus said they were going to run Big Mallard rapid down the right side. They almost didn't make it. Mark, a bit wiser now, rowed the other boat down the left side of the rapid, "where you are supposed to run Big Mallard." He'd just learned that Bus was still willing to try the worst places. The Middle Fork of the Salmon became a standard offering in the Hatch River Expeditions catalog by the 1960s.[13]

The same year, Bus returned to another old haunt, the Grand Canyon. Frank Hatch had run a 10-man raft equipped with an outboard through the Canyon in 1948, but Bus had not been back since 1934. In April of 1954, he took another group from Colorado, this one organized by Tyson Dines, a Denver banker. Dines had floated the Yampa with Bus two years before, and in 1953 they ran the Green all the way from Gates of Lodore to Green River, Utah. On the latter trip, Dines amazed even the old river rat by standing on his head, while paddling his 18-foot aluminum canoe through a rapid. Bus was impressed. When Ty suggested that he'd like to try the Grand Canyon, Bus said he had been thinking of expanding the business to include trips on the Colorado, and besides, he'd like to see the Grand Canyon again, since it had been twenty years. Bus and Ty worked out a deal. Bus would provide the boats, crew, and expertise. Dines could bring anyone he wanted, would arrange transportation and supplies, and do the cooking.[14]

Bus brought an oar-powered pontoon, and a ten-man raft with a small outboard motor. Smuss Allen, another old friend of Bus's, offered to row the pontoon for free, since he had never used one—nor had he ever been down the Grand Canyon. Bus, Frank Hatch, and Ty Dines were in the ten-man raft. The water was low. About mile 130 is Bedrock Rapid, a sharp turn to the right around a block of granite as big as a house. It looks much easier to run than it is. As so many have since, Smuss misjudged the run and crashed into the rock. The big pontoon slowly slid under the edge of the massive boulder, as he and the passengers scrambled up onto the sloping surface. Bus saw what was happening, so he and the others in the ten-man motored back and forth in the big eddy below, retrieving gear that had been torn from the big boat. Only a banjo, a case of scotch, and a 16mm movie camera was lost.

Les Jones, who was running the canyon solo in his homemade canoe, caught up to them at that point. The current was so strong that they couldn't budge the pontoon, but by prying with the oars, they were finally able to free the big boat. When it surfaced, Smuss Allen saw it departing without him and jumped from the top of the rock, expecting to land in the bottom of the boat. To his surprise, he went right through the bottom and into the river. The constant pounding of the river against the rock had ripped the bottom out of the full length of the boat. They spent the rest of the day sewing the floor back together, and finished the trip on schedule at Lake Mead. Bus later reported that he had had a "smooth trip."[15]

Bus took several Sierra Club groups through the Grand Canyon in 1956, and made the run a regular part of his business. On one of those, in April, several of the passengers were tossed from the boat in Grapevine Rapid. No one was hurt, but all were wet and scared. In 1959, he took Glade Ross along on his first Grand Canyon trip as boatman. The duffle was piled so high in the middle of the boat that Glade couldn't see where he was going, and had to depend on Bus's arm signals for guidance. Glade later wrote that he had the same problem George Wilkins described—the duffle was piled so high that he couldn't see, and he mistook Bus's talking with his hands to the passengers for arm signals.[16] This time the consequences were a little more severe, as Bus recounted in a letter written that winter.

We had an upset in a minor rapid just before reaching Lake Mead. It might be chalked up to carelessness or mebby it was just one of those things which happen so often on the river. "Hardtack" Ross was running the motor. I was sitting dumbly on the rowers seat quite content, the oars parked up at the sides. We were through the higher waves and at the end of the rapid. He got a bit far to the right and in the back eddy at the right side. He turned the boat to come back out in to the current and as he came out the boat came sidewise onto a sloping rock which was practically on the shore line. It sloped up at an even, smooth angle. The boat slid easily and slowly up until it was caught by the water coming in on the upper side and slowly rolled over. That damn rock was made perfect for a turn table.[17]

Despite these mishaps, there was still a great deal of public demand for trips down the Grand Canyon, and Bus made it a standard listing in his catalog of river trips. The cost was steep for those days—$300 per person—but Bus often took groups from the Sierra Club of up to seventy people at a time.

In 1957, Bus had one of his strangest adventures yet, again in the Grand Canyon. The previous year, on a June morning in 1956, a TWA Constellation and a United Air Lines DC-6 met in a suddenly crowded bit of airspace, 20,000 feet over the Grand Canyon. Wreckage from the two planes fell all over Chuar and Temple Buttes, across from the mouth of the Little Colorado River. None of the 128 passengers and crew survived. The bodies were removed as quickly as possible, but the wreckage, including luggage, was left in place.[18] In the summer of 1957, a man from St. Louis named Robert Billingsley came up with a ghastly idea. Why not float down the Colorado, find the wreck site, and collect all the valuables and money surely still there? After all, he reasoned, the victims didn't need it anymore. So Billingsley did just that, floating from Lee's Ferry on two truck inner tubes tied together.

After Billingsley had been gone for a couple of weeks, his family began to get worried. The Park Service refused flatly to send a rescue party for him by boat or anything else. So Mrs. Billingsley and his brother, Paul, called on the only man who would agree to attempt a rescue of Robert Billingsley—Bus Hatch. Bus immediately agreed to go, and furthermore to charge nothing but his expenses. He rounded up Mark Garff to go along as his assistant boatman. With Paul Billingsley and a couple of other passengers aboard a pontoon, Bus launched from Lee's Ferry on Pioneer Day, July 24th. The heat was intense, and the water was the highest anyone had seen in years—the Colorado was still flowing over 60,000 second-feet, even in July.

It was a hair-raising trip. The passengers were scared to death by the high water, and several chose to walk around Hance, a particularly nasty rapid at the start of the upper Granite Gorge. Mark Garff took the front oars, Bus the back, and one of the passengers ran the motor. In the first waves, the erstwhile motor man froze in fear, and the motor sputtered and went dead. Bus and Mark were barely able to get the boat to shore. As they waited for the passengers to catch up, Mark climbed above the boat, and dislodged some rocks and cactus. The resulting fall punctured the boat in several places, which caused Bus to "cuss for an hour." They ran the ten miles down to Phantom Ranch in less than an hour, and pulled in to ask the ranger if there was any word on Billingsley. It turned out that he had already made his exit from the Canyon, by the North Kaibab trail.[19] At any rate, there was no need for Bus to continue down river, so they rolled the boat up, stashed it below Bright Angel Creek, and arranged for mules to carry them out of the canyon.

Two things were evident to all who were there that hot July day at the bottom of the Grand Canyon. One was that the formerly good relations with the Park Service that Bus had enjoyed for years were turning sour. The ranger who met Bus and his party chastised him for not having a permit, for trying to rescue Billingsley, for even being on the river at all. Bus blew up at the young upstart, and a nasty scene ensued. Bus and the ranger stood nose to nose, yelling at each other, until they were separated by Mark Garff. Members of the river party and the rangers's companion finally calmed the two down, but it was a portent of things to come.

Two oars-men, one big boat

The other thing that was painfully evident was that Bus was not a well man. Like all of his family, he suffered from high blood pressure, and all during the trip he'd had bad nosebleeds and intense headaches. After they decided to discontinue the trip, the party headed out to the North Rim of the Grand Canyon on muleback. Mark Garff chose the last place in line, behind Bus, so that he could catch him if he fell off the mule. Bus was by this time having fainting spells as well, and Garff was convinced that he was going to die.

But Bus was, for now, too tough to die. They made it back to Vernal all right, and after some rest in the hospital, Bus was able to resume his building schedule, and run trips on the Yampa and Green, his favorite places. In 1960, he had a real surprise when his old buddy Jim Orr wrote from Alaska. Orr, who had cancer and knew his time was limited, contacted Bus to plan a river trip on the Yampa. Bus was delighted, and the spring trip was a great success. There was good fishing, and every night around the campfire Bus and Jim tried to top each others lies, and told story after story on each other. Bus rejoiced in the company of his old friends.

By 1960, Bus felt he had already done more in his life than any of his sons would ever possibly do. There were still challenges to be faced, however, and they were of a kind that Bus had neither time nor patience for. For now the river was changing, like the country was changing. The increased publicity given to Dinosaur and the national parks by the Echo Park Dam controversy had also brought increased government attention, and the spotlight of regulation was turned on the hitherto obscure canyons of the Green and Yampa. Rather than face bad rapids and impassable canyons, now faced the prospect of having someone tell him when he could or couldn't run his beloved river. To run this regulatory rapid was to be Bus's final challenge—one that he would, in the end, pass on to his successors.

endnotes

1 The dam remained a dream in the hearts of many in Vernal, however, and even today emotions run strong among older townspeople. If you go to any of the cafes in Vernal where local old-timers gather for breakfast, and bring up the subject of the Echo Park Dam, you will very likely get an argument about it.

2 One one of these trips, in 1958, Frank Swain ran a 10-man raft through Disaster Falls in Lodore without capsizing. He had never before run it successfully, and for the rest of his life was proud of finally making it through right-side-up.

3 DeSpain Rock, at the bottom of Moonshine Rapid in Split Mountain Canyon, is named for a 1953 incident in which a boat run by Roy was wrapped around the rock. No one was injured in the wreck.

4 Frank and Ted both attended the University of Utah.

5 Ted Hatch interview, 13 August 1988.

6 Tom Hatch interview, 15 January 1988. Tom died in Vernal in November 2004.

7 George Wilkins interview, 4 November 1987.

8 IBID.

9 Jesse Burton was from a ranching family who lived on the upper Green River, around Little Hole, just below Flaming Gorge Dam. Burton was also a diabetic; George Wilkins remembered almost coming to blows with a passenger who accused Burton of being a drug addict after seeing him injecting insulin one morning. Burton became one of Ted Hatch's best friends, indeed a mentor, even though their ages were similar. Sadly, Burton drowned when his boat flipped in Upset Rapid, in the Grand Canyon, just a few days before Bus's death in June 1967. Although all the passengers made it safely to shore, Jesse's life jacket caught in the motor frame and he was unable to free himself. To this day, Hatch boatmen leave an inscribed pie plate—to commemorate Burton's skills as a cook—wired to the rocks below Upset

Rapid. If the plate is somehow removed, either by the Park Service or by weather, the boatmen soon replace it. The wood stove in the Hatch River Expeditions warehouse at Cliff Dwellers, near Lee's Ferry, is also named in Burton's honor.

10 Ted Hatch later told me that he felt the oars were next to useless in rapids, and that they would just let go of them and hang on.

11 The solution to this problem was cutting out the floors of the boats, suspending the frame inside the boat, and putting the motor in the stern, inside the pontoon. Hatch gave up all of its tail dragger frames by about 1975.

12 According to Bus's own account as recorded in the 1962 Fred Washburn oral interview, in 1960 Bus quit drinking altogether.

13 According to Ted Hatch, Bus also opposed the construction of the Brownlee Dam on the Main Salmon, which was built in the late 1950s.

14 Bus and Ty Dines later became the best of friends—Dines would visit whenever he passed through Vernal.

15 Notes on Les Jones scroll map, Grand Canyon, 1960.

16 Glade Ross to Otis R. Marston, 15 July 1975. Marston Collection.

17 Bus Hatch to Otis Marston, 10 December 1959. The rapid was Mile 232, still a tricky run. Commercial boatmen sometimes call it "Killer Fang Falls."

18 Some of the bodies of the victims were returned to their families, while others were buried in mass graves in Flagstaff, Arizona and on the South Rim of the Grand Canyon. The wreckage of the two airplanes, one surprisingly intact, remained in place until the late 1970s. The bits and pieces were finally removed by the Park Service and TWA. The tragedy led to the creation of the modern air traffic control system.

19 Billingsley made it to the North Rim, where he proudly showed around jewelry, singed coins and paper money that he had collected during the three days he had spent looting the bodies of the air crash. As soon as his presence was known, he was promptly arrested for desecrating a grave site, and spent six months in jail.

I've Lived Three Lives

During the term of one (1) year from January 1, 1953, to December 31, 1953, Bus Hatch, of Vernal, Utah, hereinafter referred to as the Permittee, is hereby authorized, subject to the terms and conditions contained herein, to carry on in Dinosaur National Monument the business of guiding boating parties....[1]

THIS LONG SENTENCE sums up just what was wrong between Bus Hatch and the National Park Service. To Bus, the Park Service was a relative newcomer. When he started floating the Green through the Canyon of Lodore in 1931, the Green and Yampa canyons were not even a part of Dinosaur National Monument; that designation was still seven years in the future. One thing that had attracted Bus to the river, as it still does others today, was the feeling of freedom, or release from control over your life by outside forces. A man is his own man on the river, Bus always thought, and now here was the Park Service telling him he had to have a permit to run the Green River. Bus was disgusted.

But things hadn't always been so. For many years Bus and the National Park Service had enjoyed the best of relations. As early as 1938, the year Dinosaur National Monument was expanded to include the canyons of the Green and Yampa,[2] Bus had taken a group of scientists and Park Service officials down the Green River for a survey, and during World War II, on several occasions, Bus was called on to serve as guide and boatman for archeologists, biologists,

127

and reclamation engineers. During the Echo Park Dam controversy, Bus and his son Don had been among the few allies the Park Service could count on among the residents of Vernal for support in fighting the dam. Among the many people that Bus took down the river in that turbulent period were two very influential men in the National Park Service itself. One was Horace Albright, the director emeritus of the Park Service, and one of the founding fathers of the Service in 1916. Although he was recently retired, his word carried a great deal of weight within the Park Service and the Department of the Interior. Albright took a day trip from Echo Park down to Island Park with Bus. He felt that Bus was an active ally in the effort to stop the flooding of the canyons, and foresaw that the publicity Bus got would do great things for Hatch River Expeditions: "Apparently we have the Echo Park Dam licked, but I am sure that there will be ever increasing numbers who want to go down the river with you and your associates."[3] The other Park Service official was Conrad Wirth, at the time director of the National Park Service. He was a passenger on the March, 1953 trip down the Yampa that was showcased in *National Geographic* magazine.[4]

But Bus's association with the National Park Service, especially in Dinosaur National Monument, went far beyond hauling boatloads of dignitaries down the river. Hatch River Expeditions was a very real presence in Dinosaur from the early 1940s on. As visitation on the river increased dramatically in the 1950s, the Park Service began to develop the Monument to accommodate tourists. This included designated riverside camps with picnic tables, outhouses, water wells, and fire pits. The Park Service had no boats of its own, nor any staff experienced in handling a boat in rough water, so they hired Bus Hatch and his crews whenever maintenance work needed to be done along the river. A good example of the close ties that Bus had with Jess Lombard, Superintendent of Dinosaur in the 1950s, is the storage shed at Jones Hole. Bus and his crews hauled in the materials and then built the shed. Hatch crews used it for many years, and always considered that it was as much their shed as the ranger's.[5]

Mark Garff remembered hauling six fiberglass outhouses down Lodore in the spring of 1957. They nested together so they could be hauled on a boat and were to be placed in camps along the river. The water was so high that year and the current so fast that they couldn't get the big pontoon over in time to land at Rippling Brook, and that outhouse had to wait until later in the season.[6] In 1958, the Park Service decided to drill water wells at the camps along the Yampa. They hired a drilling crew with a small portable drilling rig, which Jesse Burton hauled down the river on a 27-foot pontoon. He then stayed with

the crew as camp cook and helper all summer while they drilled the wells.

In August of that same year, Bus sent George Wilkins by himself to take a load of drill pipe, casing, drill bits, and sacks of cement down to the drilling crew. The water was low by then, and the trip was arduous. What Bus thought would take three days took twice as long; in a couple of places, Wilkins had to wade out into the river and build wing dams out of rocks to make a channel deep enough to float the pontoon. After he was overdue for a couple of days, Bus hired a light plane to go look for him. Wilkins, camped at Five Springs Draw, saw the plane pass overhead, and waved. On the next pass, it was right down in the canyon. Bus threw out a duffle bag with a parachute attached, but the plane was so low that the bag smashed into the hillside above Wilkins's camp. George scrambled up the hill to retrieve it—getting tangled in a patch of cactus along the way—and found that the bag contained cookies, a loaf of bread, and cans of sardines and spam. Tom Hatch, who had packed the bag, knew that Wilkins hated sardines and spam, and the cans had reduced the bread and cookies to tiny crumbs upon impact. In the bag was a note from Bus, giving arm signals for Wilkins to use if he was hurt or needed help. It was not recorded just what kinds of arm signals George gave. He threw the sardines in the river, and used the spam as bait to catch catfish. He also used the parachute to make a sail, which worked well when the wind was right. When he finally got to the Mantle Ranch, Mrs. Mantle fed him a huge breakfast; once he got to the Green, there was enough water to finish the journey without further problems. Another crew, which had left after him, abandoned the attempt and cached their boat and equipment.

Bus and his crews were often called on to fight fires within the Monument, as an article in *Desert Magazine* noted:

> A lightning bolt started a fire on the steep slopes of Split Mountain Canyon in Dinosaur National Monument. Jess Lombard, monument custodian, scouted the blaze by airplane and found that it was inaccessible by foot or horseback. So, piloted by Bus Hatch, veteran river runner, Lombard and Lee Sneddon, park ranger, traveled by boat up the Green River, 3½ miles into jagged Split Mountain Canyon, landed, and had the fire out by nightfall.[7]

Not only did Bus and his crews carry Park Service personnel into areas that were accessible by other means, they would often actively help fight the blaze.

Another job Bus and his men were often called on was rescue and recovery. As more and more people began to run the river on their own, there were inevitably accidents and even some drownings. Whenever there was a person missing on the river, Bus would either send men and equipment to aid in the search, or would at least loan boats to the searchers. For neither of these services, fire fighting or rescue and recovery, did Bus ask for or receive any pay from the National Park Service. As far as he was concerned, the rangers and other personnel were just part of the family, and Dinosaur was home.

Dinosaur was not the only place that Hatch crews and boat were called on for service only they could provide. The same applied as well in the Grand Canyon and in Cataract Canyon. Bus even sent boats to aid fire crews battling blazes along the Salmon River in Idaho. As with the rangers in Dinosaur, Bus had a very good rapport with the rangers in Grand Canyon National Park. In the early 1950s, when Bus was going to take a trip, it was enough to call Lynn Coffin, the ranger at Lee's Ferry, and tell him that he was bringing a party down the river. There was no written permit system then.

But when the Park Service began to require formal permits to run the river in the mid-50s, relations with Bus took a turn for the worse. In his report about the Billingsley affair, Park Ranger Daniel Davis noted what Bus thought of permits:

Because Hatch has always been in the habit of writing in for a permit about the time he left Vernal for Lee's Ferry making it impossible for us to get the permit to him in time, and because he would not use our application forms which we consider vital information needed before a permit can be issued, we wrote him several years ago requesting that he get his application in six weeks early because every year it would take several letters to get the required information out of him. He normally uses the Dinosaur form which asks for none of the information which is considered necessary through Marble and Grand Canyons.[8]

Permits weren't the only regulations that Bus had to deal with. Even before the permit system was instituted, the Park Service began requiring concessionaires—and in Dinosaur at the time, concessionaires automatically meant Hatch River Expeditions—to carry liability insurance. In March 1954, Jess Lombard wrote to Bus about the problem, telling him almost apologetically "What this boils down to, Bus, is the National Park Service can not accept responsibility of your operation as a concession if you are not fully covered by liability insurance."[9] It's easy to imagine Bus's feelings about this development.

The final blow, at least in Bus's eyes, came in the early 1960s. During the 1953 trip down the Yampa with *National Geographic*, Park Service director Conrad Wirth effusively praised Bus and his operation, and told Bus that if he kept up the good work, he would have the only legal concession in Dinosaur National Monument. In effect, Wirth was promising Bus a monopoly on commercial river running on the Green and Yampa. For many years, Bus and Hatch River Expeditions did in fact hold the only legal concession on the Monument. Had Wirth been able to keep his promise, such a monopoly would have been a gold mine, especially when river running skyrocketed in the late 1960s.

Alas for Bus, such favors were not really in Wirth's power to grant. Even at that early date, there were others who were starting in to the river running business. They took semi-private, cost-sharing trips down the river that were actually thinly-veiled commercial enterprises. It was only natural—there was a growing demand, and Bus couldn't fill all of it, so others stepped in. These special-use permittees, as they were called, were cutting in on Bus's business and doing it without the paperwork that went with holding a concession. Bus had to file rate schedules, financial reports, and statements of liability, and had to pay use fees for holding a concession. It was the price he paid for being the first concessionaire. The holders of special-use permits had to do none of these things. By the early 1960s, there was so much competition that Hatch River Expeditions had to advertise for the first time. Finally, in 1962, Jack Currey founder of Western River Expeditions, sued the Park Service, claiming that they had illegally granted Hatch a monopoly. Currey won the suit and was granted a concession.[10]

In none of this was Hatch River Expeditions singled out. The 1950s and early 1960s were a period of great changes in how the Park Service managed the national parks. Concession contracts in all parks and monuments were reviewed, and made to more strictly follow the Park Service's new guidelines. But to Bus, who remembered the old days when it was an occasion to even see another party on the river, the idea of filling out forms and paying fees to run the river was all but unbearable. It was all too evident to Bus that the free and easy days he had known for so long on the river were over. Consequently, he began to lose interest in the day-to-day running of the river business, and turned more of the details over to his sons Don and Ted. It was one thing to go down the river with your buddies, drinking moonshine, hunting and fishing; but it was quite another dealing with insurance, regulatory agencies.

and competitors, all clamoring for your attention or a share of the action. One former boatman remembered that during the early 1960s, Bus would sometimes pick up the mail at the house. If there was a letter from Jim Orr or Dock Marston or some other old crony, Bus would simply leave the rest of the correspondence wherever he sat down to read the letter. Someone would find the rest of the mail, often containing hundreds of dollars in deposit checks for river trips, blowing around the yard a few days later.

Other changes were taking place in Bus's life as well. Bay Hatch was the first of his immediate family to pass away, in 1950. Then Eva died unexpectedly of a stroke in January 1962, leaving Bus alone. Jim Orr died of cancer in Alaska the next year. Tom and Alt were still alive, but both lived far from Vernal, as did Frank Swain. In 1964, Bus remarried, after first going to each of his sons and asking their opinions. He and his new wife, Marie Paulsen, traveled and fished in Mexico and Colorado. The values that had always been the foundations of Bus's life now took on new meaning. His family was as important as ever, and he took real delight in his many grandchildren. His love of the outdoors, of fishing, hunting, and just being in the hills and canyons near Vernal had never left him, and he found more and more joy in being outdoors as he grew older.[11]

Because of failing health, Bus quit running the river in 1964. Now it was obvious to him more than anyone else that he was just waiting for the end. His heart was bad, and he suffered from arthritis in his feet, from standing in cold rivers for so many years. Bus was still a fighter, though, and even if he wasn't going down the river he was still involved in the business in other ways. In a letter written to Don and his son Frank just months before he died, Bus noted that the new oars he had ordered had come in, and he was going to oil and varnish them himself. In the same letter, he made a rare reference to his health: "I have been layed up for a while with sinus and arthritis in both feet. It sure has been hell. The sinus is better but old Arthur and I are having a hell of a battle."[12] He and Marie moved into a smaller house down the street, that was easier to heat, and Bus spent the cold winter months sitting by the stove, thinking about the old days.

Finally, in June, 1967, just as the box elder trees were leafed out along the Yampa, just as the geese were finishing their flight north along the river, Bus's health began to deteriorate badly. He was hospitalized in Vernal, suffering from extreme high blood pressure and a failing heart. His son Ted went to visit him, and as he looked at his father in the hospital bed, Ted began to cry. Bus gave him a sharp look. "What the hell are you crying about, son?" "It looks like you're not going to make it, Dad," Ted replied. "Jesus Christ son-

of-a-bitch, son!," Bus bristled, "don't cry for me, cry for yourself. I've lived enough for three lives in my time. You'll never do half the things I've done in my time." Somehow, Ted remembered, the old flash of temper made him feel better about his father's end.[13] Bus lived only a few more days. He died peacefully on June 17, 1967, and was buried in the Vernal Cemetery.

e n d n o t e s

1 National Park Service Concession Permit, 1953.

2 Dinosaur became a National Monument in 1915, but that only applied to about 80 acres around the dinosaur quarry near Jensen, Utah. It was not until 1938 that President Franklin Roosevelt designated about 230,000 acres, including the Green and Yampa canyons, as Dinosaur National Monument.

3 Horace Albright to Bus Hatch, 28 December 1955.

4 "Shooting Rapids in Dinosaur Country," by Jack Breed. *National Geographic*, March 1954, p. 363-392. For more on Bus and the Echo Park Dam controversy, see Chapter 4.

5 Another indication was that Frank Hatch married Jess Lombard's daughter. For a while in the 1970s, the Park Service tried to restrict Hatch crews from using the shed, but finally conceded that the shed belonged to Hatch as much it did to them, and gave the keys to Don Hatch.

6 In the late 1970s, I helped haul those outhouses out when they were replaced with simple wooden shields. The outhouses, picnic tables, and fire grates were all taken out by the early 1980s, and the campgrounds today are wilderness-style. All waste must be taken out by the boating party.

7 *Desert Magazine*, October 1947

8 "Memo to Chief Ranger, Grand Canyon National Park, from Supervisory Ranger Davis, 5 August 1957."

9 Jess Lombard to Bus Hatch, 25 March 1954.

10 In the 1970s, under the River Management Plan, the NPS made all holders of special use permits into *de facto* concessionaires, and froze the number of concessions granted within the monument at thirteen. At the time, based on prior usage, Hatch

River Expeditions was given the greatest share of the allotted boater-user-days.

11 Another change occurred on the Yampa River, one of Bus's favorite stretches, about two years before his death. On the evening of June 10, 1965, a major flash flood came down Warm Springs Draw, about four miles above Echo Park, and turned Warm Springs Rapid, which had been little more than a riffle, into a difficult and even dangerous rapid. Indeed, the first boatman through it, Les Oldham, who was leading a Hatch two-boat trip of Boy Scouts, was thrown from boat and drowned. Warm Springs has been the scene of many accidents and even drownings since; it is not known if Bus ever ran Warm Springs but given his age and health, it's unlikely.

12 Bus Hatch to Frank and Don Hatch, March 1967.

13 Ted Hatch interview, 13 August 1988.

We've set river running back twenty years

FOR THE HATCH FAMILY, the decade after Bus's death in 1967 was the proverbial best of times and worst of times. The publicity that the company garnered from the Echo Park Dam controversy made them a household name, which in turn brought some high profile clients, thereby bringing even more publicity. It was a spiral to the top of the river running world that lasted for some years. At the same time, some of their most valued and loyal customers would walk away from Hatch, as a result of outside pressures from the burgeoning environmental movement of the 1960s. The same people and organizations that stopped the Echo Park Dam and would save the Grand Canyon from dams started to question the very way that Hatch ran their trips, and in the end tried to force them to change. Don and Ted, who by now were the ones running the business, were not willing to change and as a result lost those customers forever. Finally, the stresses of running what became the largest river outfitting company in the country eventually caused a split between brothers that would have troubled Bus—to whom family was everything—a great deal.

The Hatch family had gotten used to publicity during the Echo Park Dam controversy, but starting in 1965, high-profile clients brought national attention to their corner of Utah, and to the river trips that they ran. That year Robert F. Kennedy, Senator from New York and brother of the slain president, contacted Hatch about taking his family and others down the Yampa and Green Rivers through Dinosaur National Monument. The trip was fairly low-

key for the Kennedys, whose family vacations sometimes resembled a traveling circus. The next year they came back to run the Middle Fork of the Salmon in Idaho. This time they brought along a number of their ten children and some other family members, as well as family friends Senator John Glenn, Jim Whittaker, the first American to climb Mt. Everest, skier Willy Schaeffler, actress Claudine Longet, and various others It was a wonderful trip, although Don and Ted were not used to clients who were accustomed to being waited on. As one of the boatmen on the trip, Al Holland, noted, the Hatches were not ready for luxury trips, but they adapted:

> They conceived that they'd invented river running and their dudes needed to learn to do things the Hatch way. They got grumpy when the kids didn't wash their own dishes. Nonetheless, Don and Ted flew in extra ice and alcohol at Flying B. For the first time ever they made valiant efforts to offer a luxury trip. Ted and Don did not understand how important personal service was to a successful trip, especially a trip booked by a family accustomed to professional service. They resented rendering personal service. Ted took personal affront to "the Senator's" call "beah heah" each time he wanted another beer during the day, yet Ted was ever-ready with another cold one.[1]

138   Riverman

The Kennedy family trips were not about quiet contemplation of the wilderness; rather, they were marked by arduous hikes, jumping off cliffs, swimming rapids, and general rambunctiousness. Water fights were another favorite pastime, on the boats during the day and even in camp. Ted Hatch remembered that at one point, a furious water fight broke out while they were on the river. John Glenn was riding with Ted and they were on the losing end of the fight.

> We got in a water fight, and the Kennedys were just poundin' us. They had all the buckets, and we were in rowboats, and John said, "Get closer to 'em. I know how to fix this." I said, "John, they're whippin' our ass, we gotta get across the river, get away from 'em." "No," he said, "get over there." So I got closer, and he dove in, swam across, got in the boat with Ethel and the Kennedy kids. He grabbed each one of 'em and threw 'em in the river. Threw 'em all out! And then I went over and picked him up, and we went back and he said, "That'll slow 'em down." "What made you think of that?" He said, "It's an old Marine tradition to charge when you don't know what to do."[2]

The Kennedy family had such a good time that they came back to float the Grand Canyon with Hatch in 1967. For the Grand Canyon trip, Robert and Ethel Kennedy once again brought along a large following, this time including singer Andy Williams, Jim Whittaker, writer George Plimpton, Willy Schaeffler, family friend Lem Billings (inventor of "Fizzies"), humorist Art Buchwald, and "350 Kennedy children," according to Buchwald.[3] Actually there were 42 people in the party, not counting crews for the six pontoons. The boatmen included Don and Ted Hatch and several of their most experienced boatmen such as George T. Henry, Jack Jukes, and Walter Kirschbaum.[4]

The Kennedy family was the closest thing to American royalty, and they were treated like it. Not only did they bring an entourage, they had mountains of duffle. Even though this was a time of low flows in the Grand Canyon, because Lake Powell was still filling up, while they were on the river the water came up and stayed up. On a couple of occasions airplanes flew down the canyon past their camps, and dropped blocks of ice for cocktails and cold drinks. Warren Herlong, a 19-year old college student from Alabama, was a swamper on the trip and remembered that one of his jobs was the fish the ice out of the river and chip pieces off for drinks. There was a boatload of reporters along to provide publicity, although they camped on different beaches.[5] Things almost got off to a bad start, though; as they approached Badger, the first rapid, Bobby Kennedy declared his intention of swimming through the rapid on his air mattress. Ted Hatch, appalled by the thought of losing a member of the Kennedy family on the first day, warned him not to try it, as Badger is a big rapid. Kennedy would not be told what to do, and besides, as George Plimpton noted, "Taking an icy dip before lunch was a WASP ritual… you would let out a gleeful whoop and then down a martini."[6] Kennedy dove in, the air mattress went one way, he went another, and he was pounded by the big waves. When they finally caught up to him, quite a way downstream, he was exhausted and beat, but the first thing he did when he was pulled back into the boat was apologize to Ted for not taking his advice. Whenever they wanted to swim a rapid after that, they always asked first. According to all accounts, it was a great trip. At night Andy Williams would sing, Art Buchwald would tell funny stories, or there might be a football game between the Kennedys and the Hatch crew. The fun was fueled, in part, by copious quantities of Old Fitzgerald Bourbon (the Kennedy family brand), as well as Andy William's fine French wines.

The Kennedys only went to Phantom Ranch, where they planned to climb out. But by now the weather had grown unbearably hot, and Ethel, concerned about the younger children, wanted to fly them and some others out from

140

Phantom Ranch. Once they stopped there, she telephoned the superintendent of Grand Canyon and asked for a helicopter. She was told that there was no way a helicopter would be allowed. Undeterred, she made another phone call, and the next day a helicopter appeared to fly the youngest children out. The rest were left to climb out the Bright Angel trail, a seven-mile hike that gains almost a mile of altitude. It was an ordeal for all but Bobby Kennedy, who encouraged the others by quoting the St. Crispin's Day speech from Shakespeare's *Henry V*.[7]

Even though the Kennedys had only gone part way through the Grand Canyon, the resultant publicity was a boon not only for the Hatch business but for river outfitters in general. Ted Hatch later noted that their phone didn't stop ringing for months after the trip, and Hatch River Expeditions was once again catapulted into the national spotlight.[8] The Kennedy family planned another trip with Hatch the following year, on the Selway River in Idaho, but before that could take place Robert Kennedy was assassinated in California on June 5, 1968. Ted Kennedy, the surviving brother, later came out to Utah and ran the Green with Hatch in 1969, but the days of the big Kennedy family trips ended with Bobby's death.

After the Kennedy trips, Hatch was busier than Bus could have ever imagined. Boats, crew, and gear were still transported from the Hatch boatyard in Vernal, even for the Idaho and Grand Canyon trips (although after 1967, the Grand Canyon passengers were met at Marble Canyon or Lee's Ferry, and the final staging was also done in Arizona). It was a long drive to and from Vernal, but that was the way things had always been done. A younger generation of boatmen was starting to lead trips, too, as the old timers, such as Glade Ross, George Wilkins, and Mark Garff, started moving on with their lives. The drowning of Shorty Burton in Upset Rapid in June 1967—coming within days of Bus's death—was a great shock to many of the older boatmen, and was a personal loss to Ted.[9] There were still family members involved, such as Gus's son Tom, and Don's sons Barry and Craig, all of whom were by this time old enough to work on the river. Other young boatmen came from all over; Dave Yeamans and Earl Perry were from New Mexico, Al Holland and his brother Bob from California. Jerry "Snake" Hughes and Curtis "Whale" Hansen were high school friends from Idaho. Others were local boys from Vernal or the Uinta Basin, like Dennis Massey, Bert Chew (also known as "Rollo," for a flip in the Grand Canyon), and Earl Staley. Jack Jukes, who was quite a bit older and much more sober than many of the Hatch hands, was from Salt Lake City. All had found their way to Hatch through different means but once they got there, they stayed for a few years—or many, in some cases—and contributed to the culture that had grown up around the Hatch boatyard.

In carrying on the tradition started by Bus, many of them were a hard-drinking, hard-living bunch, the terror of the local police and local fathers.[10] The ones from out of town lived in shacks and trailers at the boatyard, doing odd jobs such as mowing the lawns, patching boats, repairing equipment and cleaning out foodboxes, waiting for the magic words "'Pack a lunch, boys. You're going on a two-day,' or some such endearing line that meant we finally got to be boatmen." Dave Yeamans remembered that after waiting around the boatyard for weeks, he finally hid under the tarp on a trailer heading for Lee's Ferry for a Grand Canyon trip. Discovered only when the crew got there, they made him a swamper, or assistant/trainee boatman, and he worked for Hatch for a number of years.[11]

By this time, Hatch was offering trips in the Grand Canyon, the Green and Yampa, the Middle and Main Forks of the Salmon in Idaho. They still ran trips elsewhere, on the San Juan, and in Desolation and Cataract Canyons, but these became more rare as business picked up in Dinosaur, in Idaho, and in the Grand Canyon. Among the boatmen, a hierarchy developed. In a way, it was a natural division: the motorheads tended to work for Ted, while the oarsmen were more inclined to work with Don. The Grand Canyon boatmen considered themselves the cream of the crop, since the rapids there, along with the length of the trip and the harsh weather, made the trip seem so much more difficult. They would brag that the only true boatmen were those who could

run a motor rig through the Grand Canyon, and they usually didn't have to do drudge work of cleaning food boxes or patching boats. On the other hand, those who preferred rowing boats felt that they were the elite, and gravitated to the Middle Fork of the Salmon and the Green and Yampa in Dinosaur, where the trips were shorter, the conditions weren't quite so harsh, and there didn't seem to be quite so many characters among the crew.

One boatman from the era who ran in the Grand Canyon remembered that "a Hatch boatman had the power of life and death (or we thought we did) and it affected some of the guys adversely... egos the size of Montana... hatchlings or hatchmates or some unprintable things we were called... and we were the baddest asses on the river... just look at the ugly colors of hatch boats... Halloween orange, black and silver... some added painted teeth on the front... they were like a high school fraternity who wanted to fight everyone (and when nobody was willing, they often fought each other)."[12] Although not every boatman was a miscreant, there were enough bikers, hometown bullies, drunks, and jumpy Vietnam vets to make a self-described "sheltered, deep South, cleancut, very polite" young college student like Warren Herlong wonder what he had gotten himself into.[13] Grand Canyon boatmen boasted about driving straight from Las Vegas, where the Grand Canyon trips ended up, drinking beer the whole time, getting back to the boatyard in Vernal and going out on another trip the next day.[14] Hatch boatmen at the other end brought life to the sleepy little town of Stanley, Idaho, where Middle Fork trips began. There was no such thing as a bad back or wrenched joint from the heavy lifting; you just shrugged it off and went on. One Hatch boatman from the 1960s remembered that in the mornings they would have pliers fights, to see who could pinch the other the worst. Pliers, were, in fact, afforded the same value as holy relics among believers; no boatman was properly dressed without a pair of pliers at his belt. Beside pliers fights, they were used for untying knots in soaked ropes, lifting lids from pots and dutch ovens from the fire, turning valves, opening cans—including beer cans, as this predates the poptop can—and picking up a coal to light a cigarette. Standard attire for boatmen then was short cutoff jeans, no shirt, and high-top tennis shoes. Sunburns? Only for the "dudes." [15]

After being on top of the river running world for so long, there didn't seem to be much reason to change the way things were done in Hatchland. They had a large supply of war surplus boats, the old cotton-fabric neoprene 10-mans for Idaho, and the bigger bridge pontoons, ranging from 27 to 33 feet, for the Green and the Grand Canyon. The 10-man rafts were ideal for smaller rivers, and needed little in the way of modification. As they aged and the material deteriorated, however, it became increasingly difficult to keep them in good enough shape to be safe to use on the river. For instance, many of the old rafts had an inflatable ring around the outside of the tube, which was supposed to serve as a splashguard. After a while these tubes suffered so many punctures and tears that they would no long hold air, so in a flash of ingenuity typical of Hatch boatmen, who had often heard the saying "We'll fix it on the river, boys!," the boatmen threaded a piece of steel rebar into the tube, making a great place to tie a bow rope. [16] Otherwise, the old rafts were used on the Middle Fork and Selway, and for smaller trips on the Green and Yampa, well into the 1970s, when manufacturers started making rafts that could stand up to the rigorous use they would get from a river outfitter.

The pontoons were rigged much the way they had always been rigged since the company started using them after World War II, with two sets of oars for the Green and an outboard motor added for the Grand Canyon (although at this time, motors could still be used in Dinosaur as well). There was a wooden frame with two sets of oarlocks, with a floor made of wood or iron grillwork, suspended from the frame by chains. This was used both on the upper river and in the Grand Canyon. To rig the motor, they used the notorious tail-dragger, in which the motor was suspended on an A-shaped frame that extended off the tail of the boat. The original rubber floors were left in the boats in the Grand Canyon for years. With a motor, this made them faster and they could turn much more quickly. They could also be made more stable for big rapids by dumping in gallons of water; Ted Hatch remembered pouring in as much as

fifty 5-gallon buckets of water to stabilize the boat before Lava Falls. However, when there was no water in the bottom, and especially when there was a huge duffle pile in the middle of the boat, they were dangerously unbalanced. By the early 1970s, other companies in the Grand Canyon were starting to put outrigger side tubes on their boats for stability. Hatch occasionally used them for trainee boatmen, although the experienced hands derisively called these "training wheels." But after a number of embarrassing and expensive flips, in which boats and equipment were damaged and people had to be evacuated from the river, Hatch finally started using side tubes, the last company in Grand Canyon to do so.[17] The frames or the suspended floors would often fail under the stresses of big rapids, as would the other wooden parts, necessitating new parts being sent in to Phantom Ranch or in some cases, riverside repairs. The methods of carrying the kitchen and other gear, as well as the passenger's

duffle, remained the same for both types of boats. All gear was placed in the stern of the rafts, and in the middle of the pontoons, on top of a huge waterproof tarp. The tarp was then folded over the pile, and the whole thing was tied down using yards of rope, with knots and hitches that would make a mule packer envious. By the end of the trip, the knots had tightened so much that it was impossible to work them loose, so every boatman carried a sharp knife to cut the ropes. It was wasteful, but this was before the days of easily-available straps and buckles. Like many outfitters, Hatch stashed gas cans at various places along the river, and almost all of the trips went all the way out to Temple Bar, on Lake Mead.

By the early 1970s, Hatch was the largest and best known outfitter on the whole river, but things beyond their control were changing to the point that the company was forced to respond. Before his death, Bus had been disgusted by the increasing regulation required by the various government agencies that managed the rivers; afterwards, it only got worse, from the company's point of view. One major change was the introduction of licensing requirements for boatmen. In the old days, all you really needed was a strong back and a willingness to work hard, but after a series of tragic incidents in the 1960s involving river runners in Utah, in which numerous lives were lost, the state stepped in and imposed regulations on the river companies.[18] This included a license requirement, and Utah regulators came up with a test that boatmen had to pass before they would be granted a license to operate a raft on a river. Ted Hatch was one of the first to pass the test, holding Utah guide license #007. At the same time, he got a copy of the answers to the test and posted them on the wall of the warehouse, warning his boatmen that they had to miss a few to make it look good. The National Park Service in Grand Canyon followed suit some years later, as did the U.S. Forest Service in Idaho.

Another change was increased competition. Hatch had had competitors as far back as the early 1960s and even before, but in the early 1970s, interest in the river—and thus interest in taking paying passengers down the river—exploded. In Dinosaur, among others there was ARTA, which was started by Lou Elliott in California in 1963; Holiday River Expeditions, founded by Dee Holladay; Harris-Brennan, started by Don Harris and Jack Brennan; and George Wendt, who later founded OARS, Inc. Ron Smith founded Canyonlands Expeditions and Grand Canyon Expeditions in the early 1970s, directly competing with Hatch on both the Green and the Colorado, as did Moki Mac, founded by the family of Al Quist. Georgie White, the self-styled "Woman of the River," ran trips on the Green and Colorado and billed herself as a low-cost alternative to Hatch's trips. There were also a number of established outfitters in Idaho who expanded their river running operations around the same time. Don and Ted were charter members of the Western River Guides Association, Don serving as its president, but the increasing competition for business only meant that much more stress on the two brothers.

But it was a development in the middle of the 1970s that shook Hatch River Expeditions to its core. In the late 1960s, the Bureau of Reclamation announced plans to build two dams in the Grand Canyon. The Sierra Club, which had worked with Hatch to defeat the Echo Park Dam in the 1950s, immediately announced their opposition to this idea, and the Hatch family was right behind them. After an acrimonious debate, the proposal was defeated. Don and Ted Hatch felt they had supported the Sierra Club in this battle, and were glad to see the Grand Canyon protected. Within a few years, however, the Sierra Club and Hatch would become adversaries in another fight, this time over the idea of using motors on boats running the river through the Grand Canyon, and the two former allies would become sometimes bitter rivals.

Hatch was blindsided by this; the Sierra Club had long been one of their most loyal and valued customers, dating back to the late 1940s. But times had changed, and the 1960s saw increasing environmental awareness. The Wilderness Act was signed into law in 1964, and many Sierra Club members began to see the

Don and Ted Hatch

Grand Canyon as a potential wilderness area. Since mechanized travel was banned in already-established wilderness areas, one of the first steps toward designation of the Grand Canyon would mean prohibiting the use of motors on river trips. Hatch, as the largest outfitter on the river in Grand Canyon and an advocate for the use of motors for safety, was squarely in their sights. The opening round was fired at a Sierra Club meeting in Mill Valley, California, in 1970, to which Don and Ted were invited by the Club's river tour director. They went expecting to talk about the trips that had already been booked for the Sierra Club; what they got instead was antagonism and pointed questions about the use of motors. Meg Hatch, Don's wife, was along and remembered that she was shocked by the hostility exhibited by the membership. The small, close-knit river community in Grand Canyon was divided as well; some advocated the use of oars only, while others supported Hatch in their fight to keep using outboards. The issue finally died down after a few years; by this time river running had become a big enough business that the outfitters had connections in Washington, and the Park Service ruled that motors could still be used. There were other reasons that the Sierra Club decided to quit sponsoring river trips, but the motors vs. oars controversy was definitely a part of their split with Hatch.[19]

Another controversy that arose shortly after the motors question died down was the allocation of permits to run the river. For many years, private individuals had neither the experience nor the equipment to run rivers on their own. River trips were, perforce, the domain of commercial outfitters. But by the middle of the 1970s, more and more people wanted to do it themselves, and equipment manufacturers responded to the need by turning out boats, oars, life jackets, waterproof bags, and other types of gear that would allow people to put together their own river trip. Just as this new generation of private river runners was ready to go, however, they found themselves shut off from the river by the new regulations that required permits to run virtually all of the whitewater stretches of the Green and Colorado, including the Grand Canyon. As part of the regulations, only so many people were allowed to run the river during the year, defined as "user-days." In the Grand Canyon, only a certain number of launches were allowed each day as well. Commercial outfitters such as Hatch, by virtue of the fact that they had been doing it for decades, were given virtually all of the user-days and the launches when the rules were put in place, effectively blocking private river runners from being able to go down the river. Individuals and smaller outfitters, who wanted a greater share of the river, objected. Again, Don Hatch found himself on the opposite side of an issue from some of the people whom he had considered long-time colleagues, acquaintances, even friends. Hatch, as the largest and certainly the best known outfitter, was perceived among the private river running community as being responsible for obstructing a fair division of access to the river. Whether this was true or not, Don and Ted Hatch were never ones to back down from a fight and they felt that their business, which their father had started decades before, was being threatened. After an exchange of heated correspondence and even more heated meetings between all parties that dragged on for several years, the Park Service eventually changed their allocations to allow for more private river trips, but it was a compromise that left no one satisfied.[20]

All of this conflict and stress was reflected by a tension between Don and Ted that led to the ultimate break between the two. In a way, it was only natural; family members, especially siblings, do not often make the best business partners. But the Hatch family had worked together for so long, going all the way back to Bus's family construction business with his brothers and the Swain cousins, that any split between family members was seen as a much bigger problem than it really was or indeed, turned out to be. By the time that Bus died in 1967, Don and Ted were running the river business together. Their other brothers, Gus, the eldest, and Frank, the third brother, had found other careers and moved away from Vernal. Don and Ted planned the trips, packed the trips, hired crews, solicited passengers, and sometimes, as with the Kennedy trips, ran them together. They were partners for 17 years. As the business grew, however, this was increasingly difficult; there were just too many decisions to be made, too many factors to consider, too many trips on the water. And more importantly, the two brothers were, after all, different people. As noted above, a natural division began to form: Ted, who had first run the Grand Canyon in 1954, when he was 20 years old, had fallen in love with the place. He loved the vastness, the big rapids, the challenge. Don, on the other hand, had never liked the Grand Canyon as much; he preferred the cooler, shorter trips, closer to his home in Vernal, in Dinosaur and especially in Idaho on the Middle Fork of the Salmon and the Selway. As Ted explained the split in a 2003 interview,

> [Don] wanted to always buy new equipment for Idaho, and I wanted to buy new equipment for Grand Canyon, 'cause I loved it down here, and he loved the Idaho Salmon River country, and he loved Cataract, and he loved Dinosaur—plus it was close to his home. He wanted to stay up there... so we'd argue about equipment. Being brothers, we were rivals. We'd argue

about how to run the river, but we were best of friends. And finally one day we just decided, "You know, let's split the company. It's big, and we didn't ever dream it would be this big. Let's split the company." Of course the Idaho boats went to Idaho, and the Grand Canyon boats went to Grand Canyon. So we had a pretty good split arranged that worked out to the benefit of both of us. Then he got to be—we didn't have to go get each other's permission to buy something or to sell something, or to make big business changes, or little business changes. And we stopped having that animosity. We could call the shots. If you made a bad decision, you had to live with it. I loved the split. I always wanted to be in charge, and I was the youngest of the family, and I always had somebody tell me what to do.[21]

For a time, there was some perceived animosity between the two, but it was really more between their boatmen and adherents than between Don and Ted. After all, they were family, and family had always been important to Hatch.

Today, Hatch has been surpassed by other river outfitters, that run more trips, and have more boats, and even make more money, but no one has the name recognition that Hatch River Expeditions does. Bus Hatch, who never felt that river running was any way to make a living and support a family, would have been surprised by what the company became in the years after his death. Don Hatch died in 1994, much mourned by family and friends alike. His widow, Meg, continued to run the business until 2007, when it was sold to OARS, Inc. Ted Hatch continued to actively manage the company and even run trips in the Grand Canyon until the same year, 2007, when he retired and sold the business to one of his sons, Steve. So it's likely that there will still be a Hatch on a boat on a river in the west for the foreseeable future, and Bus would be proud of that.

endnotes

1 Personal communication, 15 November 2007.

2 Ted Hatch interview, *Boatman's Quarterly Review*, Summer 2003.

3 *Down The Seine And Up The Potomac*, by Art Buchwald. NY: G.P. Putnam's sons, 1977. p. 289-291.

4 George T. Henry was a photographer from Cedar Rapids, Iowa, who started rowing boats for Hatch in 1956 and worked for them every summer until the mid-1990s. Jack Jukes was from Salt Lake City. Walter Kirschbaum was a champion kayaker from Germany who had been a soldier in the Wermacht in World War II. Captured by the Russians at the end of the war, he spent ten years in a gulag, and came to the U.S. in 1956.

5 Ted Hatch interview, *Boatman's Quarterly Review*, Summer 2003. Warren Herlong, personal communication, 18 December 2007.

6 *American Journey: the times of Robert Kennedy*. Interviews by Jean Stein. Edited by George Plimpton. (Hartcourt Brace Jovanovich, NY. 1970.)

7 *Robert Kennedy: His Life.* By Evan Thomas. (New York : Simon & Schuster, 2000.) The speech goes, in part: "We few, we happy few, we band of brothers; for he to-day that sheds his blood with me shall be my brother; be he ne'er so vile, this day shall gentle his condition; and gentlemen in England now-a-bed shall think themselves accurs'd they were not here, and hold their manhoods cheap whiles any speaks that fought with us upon Saint Crispin's day." *Henry V*, Act IV, Scene III. Don and Ted also left the river at this point, while the boats were dead-headed (i.e., run with only crew) the rest of the way out.

8 One thing about the Kennedys that everyone noted, however, was that they did not give tips. It's not that they were cheap; they were just wealthy and powerful and were used to having people do such things for them. One family friend later said "Traveling, anywhere, just out his door, [Kennedy] was always out of cash; he never had any small change; I guess every rich man has this, but he was particularly like that." *American Journey: the times of Robert Kennedy.* p. 149

9 Both deaths occurred just days before Don and Ted were scheduled to leave on the Kennedy trip in the Grand Canyon. There was nothing else to do but carry on with the trip.

10 Jack Jukes was a notable exception to this.

11 David Yeamans, "A View From The Swamp," *Mountain Gazette* #80, May-June, 2001, pp. 52 ff. This article is highly recommended to anyone wishing to get a feel for what it was like to work on the river in those days.

12 Doc Thomas, personal communication.

13 Warren Herlong, personal communication, 18 December 2007. Herlong's rich Alabama accent so intrigued the employees of the hotel in Stanley, Idaho, that they called him "buttermouth."

14 In today's regulated, insured, and litigated river industry, such antics would mean being fired instantly, but it was a different time with different standards. Naturally, such a lifestyle took its toll on the crews, and some burned out after a few years. Others, however, stayed with Hatch for the rest of their careers, and in some cases, their lives.

15 Pliers were also used to open cans of fatty bacon in the mornings, and one boatman lost his over the side of the boat in a hitherto-unnamed rapid in Whirlpool Canyon, thus giving it the unofficial name of Greasy Pliers Rapid. The pliers were standard fencing pliers, reflecting the cowboy traditions of many of the Hatch boatmen. One former boatman noted that channel lock pliers were frowned upon, "The sort of thing that ARTA 'boatmen' would wear, if you know what I mean. Perhaps this was because channel locks could be used to lift a dutch lid without burning all the hair off your hand, and pliers couldn't." The male pronouns in this section are appropriate; there were no female Hatch boatmen in those days, and not until at least 1980 or even later in the Grand Canyon. There were a number of girlfriends who served as assistants on Grand Canyon trips, but they were unpaid.

16 Jerry Hughes, personal communication, 11 December 2007. In the summer of 2007, John Hatch, one of Don and Meg's sons, dug one of the old pontoons out of the pile of old rubber at the Hatch boatyard, somehow restored it to where it would hold air, painted it in the old Hatch colors, and took it on one-day trips in Split Mountain.

17 The most common variation, with two J-tubes, is called the S-Rig, after Rod Sanderson, an early commercial outfitter. There were many others, however, including what were called "sausage tubes" (i.e., not pointed) on either side, and double-rigs, huge boats in which two pontoons were lashed together side by side with a motor in the middle. The largest was Georgie White's G-rig, which consisted of three pontoons connected to each other by a vast network of ropes.

18 The worst accident actually occurred on the way to a river trip, not on the water. In June 1963, a large group of Boy Scouts and adults was on their way down the Hole-in-the-Rock road in southern Utah, intending to meet a river trip in Glen Canyon. The truck they were all riding in rolled over, and twelve people—four adults and eight Boy Scouts—were killed. Others were seriously injured. The group was under the auspices of SOCOTWA (an acronym for South Cottonwood Ward), a semi-

commercial river running company, which had already suffered a number of other accidents and a few deaths. It was the shock at this carnage that motivated the State of Utah to begin regulating river running as a commercial venture.

19 Another reason was that the members of the Club objected to the behavior of some of the Hatch guides. Riverside legend has always had it that Ted Hatch called his distant cousin, U.S. Senator Orrin Hatch, and had the anti-motors proposal quashed. However, since the initial round of the motors vs. oars in Grand Canyon controversy took place before Orrin Hatch was first elected in 1976, this is more than likely just rumor. The issue of banning motors from the Colorado River, however, has yet to be resolved and still causes controversy. It was one of the causes of the dissolution of the Western River Guides Association in the 1980s, and the failure of the Colorado Plateau River Guides Association twenty years later.

20 The issue of private vs. commercial river runners is another that took a long time to find a solution. Private river runners felt for many years and through many versions of the Colorado River Management plan that they were being unfairly blocked from what is, after all, a National Park that is supposed to be for all the people. Outfitters, on the other hand, felt that their businesses, which they had worked for years to build up, were being jeopardized by a change in allocations and launches. The disagreement led to lawsuits and much acrimony, and was another problem that led to the breakup of the WRGA, as noted above. However, as of this writing, a new management plan has been created that has been agreed upon by all concerned, and there is hope that the matter is settled, at least for the foreseeable future.

21 Ted Hatch interview, *Boatman's Quarterly Review*, Summer 2003. A sign of the lack of animosity between the two brothers is the fact that their offices were across the street from each other until both companies changed hands as noted in 2007. The office for Hatch Grand Canyon was in Bus's old house on 4th East and 2nd North in Vernal, while Don's office was in Cap Mowrey's old house across the street. They shared the boatyard that had once been the Hatch family homestead, until Ted built a warehouse for the Grand Canyon operations at Cliff Dwellers, Arizona, near Lee's Ferry, the starting point for Grand Canyon river trips.

Eddying Out

WHENEVER A GROUP of boatmen gets together at Ray's Tavern in Green River, Utah, or at the boat ramp at Lee's Ferry, the talk inevitably gets around to old-time river runners. They hash over whether Major Powell was a true river runner or just a bureaucrat in a boat, they argue about whether George Flavell or Than Galloway was the first to come up with the stern-first technique for running rapids, or try to settle whether Bert Loper really drowned in 24½ Mile Rapid, or had a heart attack at the head of the rapid and was already dead when his boat went over.

One name that comes up in such riverside ramblings is Bus Hatch. Few men have had such an impact on the history of river running on the Green and Colorado Rivers; fewer still have left such a heritage that is still practiced and honored today. Hatch River Expeditions is still one of the largest, and certainly one of the best known, of the commercial river operations in the West. Thousands of passengers, many of them repeat customers, go down the Green, the Yampa, the Grand Canyon, on Hatch boats. The practices, the equipment, the very esprit among the boatmen can be traced directly back to Bus. Indeed, Bus and his partners ran their boats with panache and had a great time doing it. They single-handedly turned river running from what had been a serious and even somber affair into a floating celebration, and can truthfully be said to be the spiritual progenitors of a whole generation of later boatmen.

Bus had no idea that he was creating such a tradition when he and Frank Swain and Cap and Tom paddled their new boat across the Green in 1927 to

Bus Hatch on the Middle Fork of the Salmon, 1936

Riverman

hunt geese, nor even when they took that first rough and tumble trip through the Canyon of Lodore in 1931. Bus started floating the river because he loved the outdoors, and boats were just one more way to get him into the back country that he loved so much. Being on the river was a way to spend time hunting and fishing, as well as drinking and carousing with his buddies. But as it turned out, Bus was a natural river runner. He had reflexes like a cat, and knew absolutely no fear. In the Grand Canyon on that first trip in 1934, Fred Jayne, the photographer on the trip, once screamed in fear as Bus took their boat within inches of jagged rocks in one of the rapids in the Inner Gorge. "How can you do that?" Jayne asked, shaken by the close call. "Well, I'm a carpenter by trade," Bus replied calmly. "When I cut a board I just wonder if it's going to fit. When I run a rapid like that, I just wonder if I'm going to make it."

Bus had his share of upsets, from the first rock he hit in Red Canyon in 1931, to the tragic accident on the Indus in 1956, to the capsized pontoon at Mile 232 in the Grand Canyon in 1959. But he never let it bother him, never got the shakes over a particular rapid. When you capsized, well, you just got the boat over to shore and emptied it out and tried it again; no big deal. Bus was too impatient for the careful Galloway style, preferring to row backwards into rapids, turning over, smashing the boat, laughing the whole time. He was always the first to do his share of the work, whether it was righting a boat, lining around a rapid that couldn't be run (although there weren't many of those), or patching a hole in the side of the boat. And he was the first to have his share of the joy of running rivers, whether it was the thrill of making it through a big rapid, the beauty of canyon scenery, or the comradeship of a riverside camp and a shared jug of moonshine.

Bus Hatch's list of honors in the history of river running is long. He was one of the first fifty ever to float through the Grand Canyon. He and his companions were among the first ever to run the Impassable Canyon of the Middle Fork of the Salmon. And he and Don were the first to ever run the powerful, dangerous Indus River in Pakistan, for which both were admitted into the prestigious Explorer's Club. For many years the name Bus Hatch and river running were synonymous. Whenever anyone wanted to go down the Green or the Yampa Rivers, from scientists to tourists to Boy Scouts, they thought automatically of Bus Hatch. Quite simply, there was no one else.

But Bus cared nothing for honors. The accolades of strangers meant little to him. What really mattered was the opinion of his friends and family, and even more than that, his own opinion of himself. Bus was a proud man, and rightly so, but he was never overweening in his pride. To Bus, it was enough to have

Eva and Bus Hatch

done something to the best of your ability, to know yourself that you had accomplished some personal goal. As long as you felt good about yourself, to hell with the rest of the world. When someone once asked him why he would never allow anyone to write his life's story, Bus dismissed the idea with a laugh. "It's just something to scare the kids with," he replied with a shrug.

One thing that Bus was proud of was his role in defeating the Echo Park Dam. All during that tumultuous controversy, Bus had had to keep a low profile in Vernal. His construction business depended to a great degree on the goodwill of his neighbors. At the same time, his river business depended on stopping the dams. More than just that, though, Bus hated the idea of flooding the canyons of the Green and Yampa, where he had spent so much of his life and had so many wonderful experiences, with still, stagnant water. He did everything he could to discourage the project, and in his letters to Don, who was a vocal opponent of the plan, supplied encouragement and inside information that would help defeat the project. And Bus was as happy as the rest of the town was outraged when the Dam was finally dropped from the Colorado River Storage Project.

It was during the Echo Park Dam fight that Bus built what was one of the most lasting aspects of his heritage, his place in the memories of thousands of people who went down the river with him. The Echo Park Dam was the catalyst that changed Bus Hatch going down the river with his buddies into Hatch River Expeditions. But Hatch River Expeditions would have died down with the fading fulminations of the Dam controversy if it hadn't been for Bus. During the many days and weeks he spent on the river with people from California, from back east, from all over the country that came to see what all the shouting was about, Bus kept one thing in mind. "The passengers are your bread and butter," he often told his boatmen, "so treat 'em like human beings."

And Bus truly liked people. He mixed well in any crowd, and many people that he considered acquaintances thought of him as their best friend. He loved to talk with the passengers, to tell them stories, to joke with them. His grandson Tom remembered that he viewed all the passengers on his trips as "friends he just hadn't met yet." The comments he got after the trips reflected that feeling. Glen "Brick" Johnson, coordinator for many Sierra Club trips in the 1950s, once wrote Bus that the only complaint they had after a successful season was that Bus couldn't go on each and every trip.

One reason that Bus was so well liked was that his love of the river was obvious to passengers and crew alike, and his enthusiasm was infectious. And he could make any situation, even a miserable day on the river with bugs and wind and rain seem like it was a holiday outing. "When it gets tough," Bus always said, "then you laugh." Mark Garff remembered that during the 1957 trip down the Grand Canyon to rescue Robert Billingsley, the conditions were awful. It was intensely hot, the water was high, and at one camp it began to rain. To top it off, they were caught in the middle of a hatch of beetles, and the little insects were everywhere, crawling all over them as they tried to eat or sleep. But what Mark remembered was not the heat or the rain or the bugs, but sitting under a tarp with Bus, during a driving rainstorm, and laughing for hours over Bus's stories and jokes.

But treated his passengers like friends, but he treated his boatmen like family. When he called you "son," he meant it. If one of his crew needed to borrow a car to visit a girlfriend, or some extra money to tide him over, or to be bailed out of jail, Bus was right there. "How much do you need, son?" he would ask, without any question about how the man got into the situation. The miscreant might get chewed out later, but when someone needed him, when it really counted, he knew that Bus would help him as much as he could and then do some more. At times, a passenger would take Bus aside after a trip and complain that the crew did this or that wrong, or maybe didn't treat them with proper respect. Bus would always ask his boatman "What about it, son?" If it turned out that the passenger had no real complaint, Bus would always back up his boatman, even if it meant losing that passenger's business. Family always meant more than money to Bus.

Being part of the family had its other side, as well. Bus had a quick temper, and had little patience for mistakes. When a boatman made a mistake, he would hear about it from Bus immediately. "Jesus Christ son-of-a-bitch, son, can't you do anything right?" he would roar, and the tirade would continue from there. But everyone knew that Bus's temper would soon cool, and as soon as he had made his point and made it so that the object of his anger didn't forget it, Bus would calm down and the errant crew member was part of the family again. Many former boatmen well remember the monumental ass-chewings they got from Bus, but all of them laugh when they talk about it.

But his river business and cherished memories of days on the Green or Colorado are not the only legacy left by Bus Hatch. Bus's other business, for which he is still well-known in Vernal and the surrounding towns, was as a contractor. In fact, Bus always considered himself a builder first, and a river outfitter second. Bus was in great demand as a contractor, for anyone who hired Bus to build a building, whether it was a house or a shed or an airplane hanger, knew that he would do a good job, and do it fast. Bus was famous for how quickly he could get a job done—his contracts were always on time and always under bid. Some of the buildings he left in Vernal, Moab, Salt Lake City and many other towns in Utah have been torn down, but more are still standing. Several of the large structures he built are still in use, but Bus concentrated on building homes for people to live in. Most of the fine, sturdy houses in the east end of Vernal were built by Bus and his brothers and cousins.

But perhaps Bus's most enduring legacy is that which was most important to him, his family. Like the rest of the Hatches, Bus's family ran to sons. In all of them he instilled his sense of honestly, his love of the outdoors, and his belief that a man should give a day's work for a day's wages. There are now fourth generation Hatches on the rivers of the West today, and every prospect for a veritable dynasty of river runners. All of this rests on the foundation built by Bus in those free and easy days of wooden boats in Red Canyon, the Canyon of Lodore, the Middle Fork. In his family, as in his business and his buildings, Bus Hatch built well, built to last.

A Note On Sources

MOST OF THE INFORMATION about Bus Hatch in this book was drawn from personal reminiscences of people who knew Bus. Among family members, I interviewed Don, Ted, and Frank Hatch more than once about their father and their childhoods. All of their memories were a marvelous source of not only information but a way to capture the feel of those early days in Vernal and on the river. I also talked to Tom Hatch, Gus Hatch's son and Bus's grandson, as well as Karl "Duff" Swain, who well remembered being a junior member of the construction crew in Vernal. Others who knew Bus in the early days in Vernal were Esther Campbell, Chuck Henderson, and Av Kay, while those who knew him from the river that I interviewed were Steve Bradley and Tyson Dines, both of whom went on river trips with Bus in the 1950s. Early boatmen included George Wilkins, Mark Garff, Tom Hatch, and Glade Ross, all of whom were part of the first generation of boatmen who worked for Hatch in the 1950s. I also used a number of interviews that I did some years ago while researching my first book—*If We Had A Boat: Green River Runners, Adventurers, And Explorers*, which includes a section on Bus and his early trips on the Green—for more stories about Bus. These included Frank Swain, Roy DeSpain, John Cross, Les Jones, Don Harris, and William Purdy. Finally, two oral histories that were conducted many years ago but which I was given copies were especially useful. In 1964, Vernal resident Fred Washburn invited Bus and his wife to dinner and turned on his reel-to-reel tape recorder, obtaining hours of stories. Bus's brother-in-law, Royce "Cap" Mowrey, was interviewed by Royce Hatch in 1976, and the Hatch family provided me a copy of that tape. Both of these were absolutely invaluable in re-creating those early days, and hearing Bus's and Cap's stories in their own words and own voices was a boon not often granted to a biographer.

The *Vernal Express*, the local newspaper in Vernal, was a crucial source for information about Bus and his family. Bus was well-known in Vernal and stories about his river exploits were often front page news. Other stories about Bus appeared from time to time in the Salt Lake City newspapers, such as the *Salt Lake Tribune*, the *Herald-Telegram*, and the *Deseret News*. Some of the articles about Bus came from research on microfilm, while others were clippings found in the Hatch papers at the University of Utah, or those provided by the

162

Hatch family. I did not use that many books for the simple reason that Bus was not one to care whether his name appeared in history books. An exception is Lowell Thomas's autobiography, *So Long Until Tomorrow: From Quaker Hill to Kathmandu*, which provided another side to the Indus River story. In 2000, after the first editions of this book were completed, a documentary about Cinerama was produced, which allowed me to hear Otto Lang—the director of *Search for Paradise* and a passenger on the boat that fatal day on the Indus—describe his impressions of Bus. Two other books which contain stories about Bus are *The Middle Fork and the Sheepeater War*, by Johnny Carrey and Cort Conley, which ably describes Bus's adventures on the Middle Fork and Main Salmon Rivers, and *River Runners of the Grand Canyon* by David Lavender, in which the story of the 1934 "Dusty Dozen" Grand Canyon trip can be found. The article in *National Geographic* magazine, in which Bus is profiled as well as the canyons of the Green and Yampa, is cited in the endnotes. Bus can also be seen in *Wilderness River Trail*, the film made by Charles Eggert about the Echo Park dam.

I consulted a number of manuscript sources for this book, the most interesting and useful being the private files of Don Hatch. Don rescued from obscurity—and in some cases the trash can—a great number of valuable letters, diaries, and other records of his father and other family members, and generously allowed me to use these without restriction. Manuscript sources in libraries included the papers of Russell G. Frazier, as well as early Frank Swain interviews, found in the Utah State Historical Society; and the papers of Hatch River Expeditions, Norman D. Nevills, Charles Eggert, and Roy DeSpain, in the Special Collections Department, J. Willard Marriott Library, University of Utah. I also delved into that font of information about the Green and Colorado Rivers, the Otis R. Marston papers in the Huntington Library, San Marino, California. Other tidbits came from the libraries of Grand Canyon National Park and Dinosaur National Monument, the Western History Department, Denver Public Library, and the Colorado Historical Society. A final source, but a good one, was the Regional History Room at the Uintah County Library in Vernal, Utah.

For the chapter on the history of the company after Bus died, I relied on those where were there, former Hatch boatmen Al Holland, Earl Perry, Dave Yeamans, Jerry "Snake" Hughes, Cort Conley, Pat Conley, Warren Herlong, and George T. Henry. I wanted to capture the flavor of what it was like to work for Hatch in those heady days, but I wasn't there; they were, and their memories and comments were invaluable in recreating that time.

Photo Credits

Mark Garff 91, 117

Don Hatch xiv, 3, 6A, 9, 13, 14, 31, 42, 54, 55, 60, 90, 101, 104, 103

Frank Hatch 7, 16, 17, 81

Chuck Henderson 10, 11, 28

George T. Henry 121, 138, 139

Brian Rasmussen 159

Leo Thorne 6B, 12, 63

Utah State Historical Society frontispiece, 22, 38, 39, 41, 43, 45, 47, 50, 53, 67, 70, 156

University of Utah Marriott Library 30, 64, 65, 83

Charles Neal Collection 5

Utah Power and Light Collection 24

Wes Eddington Collection 68, 69A

Wilbur Smith Collection 69B

Wayne McConkie Collection 85

Hatch River Expeditions Collection 110, 113, 115, 116, 119, 129, 131A&B, 134, 141, 142, 145, 146, 148, 158, 164, 168

THE HATCH RIVER EXPEDITIONS collection is housed in the Special Collections Department of the J. Willard Marriott Library, University of Utah. Donated by various members of the Hatch family, it consists of over 70 years of family and business correspondence, records, memorabilia, photographs, and films. It is a comprehensive resource for studying the development of not only Hatch River Expedtions, but many of the events affecting the Colorado Plateau that occurred during those decades that the company was in existence. The collection is open for research by contacting the Special Collections Department at (801) 581-8863, or by visiting the Special Collections Department website at http://www.lib.utah.edu/libraryinfo/dept/spc/

Index